THE ILLINOIS MANUSCRIPTS

THE ILLINOIS MANUSCRIPTS

VOLUME 1Z
OF
THE DRAPER MANUSCRIPT COLLECTION

Transcribed by
Craig L. Heath

HERITAGE BOOKS
2007

HERITAGE BOOKS
AN IMPRINT OF HERITAGE BOOKS, INC.

Books, CDs, and more—Worldwide

For our listing of thousands of titles see our website
at
www.HeritageBooks.com

Published 2007 by
HERITAGE BOOKS, INC.
Publishing Division
65 East Main Street
Westminster, Maryland 21157-5026

International Standard Book Number: 978-0-7884-2327-4

INTRODUCTION

The Illinois Manuscripts, Volume 1Z of the Draper Manuscripts, constitute a series of letters concerning American pioneers in Illinois, with a few original papers of Capt. James Piggott. This material was furnished to Draper (1842-68) by J. M. Peck, Isaac Newton Piggott, John Reynolds, Pierre Ménard, Benjamin Scott, James Lemen, and John T. and George Lusk. [Quoted from *Descriptive List of Manuscript Collections of the State Historical Society of Wisconsin* (State Historical Society of Wisconsin, Madison, 1906)]. A fuller description of the contents of these papers, gathered as Volume 1Z of the Draper Manuscripts in the collections of the State Historical Society of Wisconsin, is given in *Guide to the Draper Manuscripts*, by Josephine L. Harper (State Historical Society of Wisconsin, Madison, 1983).

Access to the contents of the Draper Manuscripts has been facilitated by the above *Descriptive List* and *Guide* and by documentary publications and calendars and their indexes prepared from portions of Draper's collection, as well as by the availability of the entire collection on microfilm. Nevertheless, obstacles to research in this important historical resource have remained, owing to its sheer size (491 volumes of largely handwritten documents and notes) and the lack of an index to most volumes. It is to help remedy these difficulties that the current printed transcription and index to the Illinois Manuscripts has been undertaken. It is hoped that further volumes in this series will follow.

NOTE TO USERS

This transcription of the Illinois Manuscripts was

made from the 1980 microfilm edition of the Draper Manuscripts, Volume 1Z. Portions of the documents in this volume are illegible or poorly legible, owing to fading, staining, yellowing, or tight bindings. Where illegible, these portions (whether single words or entire passages) are indicated by ellipses (...); some effort has been made to interpret poorly legible portions, but the original manuscript or microfilm copy should be consulted for verification. The transcript should be viewed as an aid to use of the manuscript, rather than a replacement or substitute for it, and users are urged to consult the original manuscript or the microfilm in parallel with the transcript.

Page numbers are handwritten on the pages of the original manuscript. These are indicated in brackets at the beginning of the text for each page in the transcript. In many cases, the beginning page of a document has a cardinal number as page number (e.g. [p. 99]), and subsequent pages in the same document have the came cardinal number with a superscript (e.g. [p. 99^1], [p. 99^2], etc.). Owing to the variability in length of text on the manuscript pages, no attempt has been made to correlate page breaks in the transcript with those in the manuscript.

The spelling, punctuation, capitalization, and grammar used in the original manuscript have been preserved so far as feasible. Dashes have generally been replaced with appropriate punctuation. In some cases, a word or phrase at the end of a line or page was repeated at the beginning of the next line or page in the manuscript; these repetitions are reproduced in the transcription.

The Table of Contents reflects Draper's division of the manuscript into sections; the section titles are either Draper's own or constitute a brief description of the section contents (e.g. "Letter" with name of addressee). Some further descriptions are included in the Table of

Contents in small typeface after the titles; these were supplied by the transcriber for the reader's convenience.

Ownership of the Draper Manuscripts by the State Historical Society of Wisconsin, and the cooperation of the Society in the production of this volume, are hereby gratefully acknowledged.

TABLE OF CONTENTS

THE ILLINOIS MANUSCRIPTS

[p. 1]
Letters from John M. Peck

Rock Spring, Illinois, Nov. 24, 1842

    Lewis C. Draper, Esq.   Dear Sir, On my return home from the Atlantic States, where I have been engaged in the Agency of the Baptist Publication Society, I found yours of May 6th.

    I am so pressed with business as to be unable at present to furnish you with any written communications on the subject you enquire about. I beg leave however to recommend to your attention the "<u>American Pioneer</u>," a Monthly Periodical 2½ sheets, with plates. This work was started last January under patronage of the "<u>Loganian Society</u>," & is conducted by John S. Williams, esq. of Cincinnati, a talented Gentleman. Its contributors are found in various parts of the West. It is devoted wholly to articles on the early settlement of our country especially the West, & chiefly original articles. I give you the contents of the last No. as a Specimen (No 10).

<u>Frontispiece</u> — Ancient mound works at Marietta, Ohio.

2. Fortifications at Marietta.   } by Daniel Stebbins &
3. Ancient Mound at Marietta } Dr. S. P. Hildreth
4. Biographical Sketch of Isaac Williams. Chap II
5. Daily Journal of Wayne's Campaign.
6. War in Virginia.
7. Toleration
8. Post office facilities from 1775 on to 1842.

The subscription price is $2.00 in advance.

   I have engaged to furnish Sketches of Boone & other articles. Mr. Williams will doubtless be very glad to receive aid from your labors.

   Very Respectfully yours &c.

J. M. Peck

Old news ... — I take some liberty in opening your letters — do you like it CHL

[p. 1¹]
Rock Spring ... J. M. Peck PM.
Nov. 25
Forwarded
Lyman C. Draper esq.
Buffalo
N.Y.
Earthquake Jan. 4th about 9 O'Clock PM

[p. 2]
Rock Spring, Illinois, Decr. 17th 1844.

   Dr. L. C. Draper,   Dear Sir, Your very acceptable letter of the 28th Nov. from Baltimore, via Philadelphia, has been forwarded to me at my residence. My private business required my attention for a couple of months & now confines me at home where I expect to be till about the last of January — My notes & Sketches of Col. Boone are scattered over my memorandum books, as I gathered them from time to time. I have published nothing. A number of facts I have furnished Rev. R. W. Griswold, Philadelphia, well known as an author, & who is engaged in compiling a more full & complete American Biography, various <u>facts</u> to correct the mistakes & misrepresentations made in the <u>Romance</u> of Flint claiming to be the Life of Boon, & also the sketch in American Biography & National Portrait Gallery. Boone was born near Bristol Pa. His parents removed to N. Carolina when he was a small boy. He never possessed the rough barbarous character one naturally attaches to a frontier hunter. He was amiable, kind, humane, prudent, sagacious, cautious & yet decidedly courageous & firm where duty called him. Many a hairbrained, madcap, who would run needlessly into danger imputed <u>cowardice</u> to Boone. He was no <u>coward</u>, but duly cautious & wary with the Indians. He certainly possessed much <u>moral</u> courage. He loved <u>nature</u> — the works of God — delighted in looking at the trees, flowers, landscape, & had the elements of poetic feeling. This, more than any delight in savage life, called him into the wilderness. He was <u>no misanthrope</u>.

[p. 2¹]
He loved his species, & had a keen innate sense of honesty, Justice, & goodness. He made no profession of religion by joining a church but he was religiously inclined, moral, & loved christian people. Most of his family connections were <u>baptists</u>. I have preached to the old man at his son-in laws, Flanders Callaway, & conversed with him for many hours. For many years he lived with Callaway who resided on the north side of the Missouri river,

near the mouth of the Charette, 40 miles above St. Charles. Boone died here of the fever Sept. 26th 182... He was about 85 years of age. His last sickness was the ... fever — bilious remittant. He lies buried on a little knoll near the bluffs. For a number of years he had ceased to hunt, as his sight had become dim. Boone's character has been much misunderstood & misrepresented by those who did not know him. The sculpture over the door leading from the rotunda to the house of Representatives in Washington is a <u>fiction</u> — no such action took place. When you get your work prepared please write me & I can furnish you with a variety of incidents. After February I shall be at the Bap. Publications office in Philadelphia for some months.

The last of October I was at <u>my</u> friend Col. Wm. Martin, Smith County Ten. & he told me of your visit & made many inquiries. I gleaned from him many reminiscences of the "olden time". The old gentleman had rode 25 miles to the Baptist Anniversaries of Tennessee & I went home with him.

I have materials for the life of the Rev. Jeremiah Vardeman, & expect to prepare & publish

[p. 2^2]
a sketch shortly — at least in the <u>Baptist Memorial</u>, & also the <u>Baptist Record</u> of Phia. in both of which the Society for which I officiate is interested. The Bap. Record is a weekly Newspaper — the Memorial a monthly pamphlet. I <u>may</u> & very likely shall work up a small <u>book</u> of Vardeman. If you can furnish me any facts from this brother I should be gratified.

I am doing very little at present in <u>writing</u> the His. of Illinois, but am gleaning materials as opportunity offers. I intend to make a labored & somewhat voluminous work of that & take time for it.

Mr. Russell is now in Louisiana Teaching. His P. O. address is <u>Clinton, East Feliciana</u>.

A young man by name of <u>Brown</u> of Chicago, has published a History of Illinois, merely a compilation & quite imperfect. It will satisfy the public till I can prepare a more full & elaborate work. No book has yet been published in the west, & very few in the east, that deserve the name of <u>The History</u> etc. They are usually partial & imperfect compilations.

You will have time to write me again to this office of which I am still <u>postmaster</u>.

In much haste, but very respectfully,
Yours &c.
<u>J. M. Peck</u>

[p. 2³]
Rock Spring Ill. <u>free</u> J. M. Peck P.M.
    Dr. Lyman C. Draper,
    Box 375, Baltimore, Md.
Dec. 17th 44
Col. D. Boone &c.

[p. 3]
Office, Amer. Baptist Publication Society,
Philadelphia, January 23rd 1846.
Dr. Lyman C. Draper. My Dear Sir, I was much gratified in the receipt of your "Circular," by this morning's mail, & for the intelligence it contains. My business will detain me in this city till the 1st May, when I leave "for good," to use a western phrase, & give place to a successor.

My time hereafter, I hope, will be spent at my own domicil, divided betwixt missionary & collateral religious services in the region arround me, & exploring & writing "Western" History. I am much inclined to think my "Illinois History," projected some years since, may turn out a General History of the Western Valley. Though your labors & mine run nearly in the same line, they will not interfere. If you make another tour to the West (& I do not see how you can help it) I hope you will not fail to visit <u>Rock Spring, Ill.</u> "You will not find the string of my door-latch pulled in." After my return I should certainly be much gratified with a visit. Very likely I have materials in my possession, you cannot obtain elsewhere. I see you propose "the life & times of Boon" amongst other projected works. I have before mentioned that I have many facts stored

[p. 3[1]]
away. The past season I have had application from Mr Sparks to prepare a Sketch of Boon for his "American Biography," which I shall accomplish soon as I return. It will not interfere with your project as it will be much condensed. I have a large mass of papers, pamphlets &c boxed up for preservation, & to which I have had no access since our correspondence for want of time to overhaul & arrange them.

On reaching my home, I shall go over all this mass of matter, & I have no doubt I can find something for you. I can part with nothing in the Western Antiquarian line, but If I knew in what you are lacking I might refer you to the sources or copy. Should you visit my domicil you can have free access & look over my materials. If you have as many old books pamphlets, newspapers &c about the <u>West</u> as my collection contains, I will then "knock under."

Have you any collections & facts about Gen. Joe. H.

Daviess, of Ky.? You know he was famous in many respects. The late Judge Rowan was his personal friend & acquaintance, & I requested him four years or more since to write Sketches of "Joe," as he was

[p. 3²]
familiary called — but I know not that he had done it before his decease. Gov. Edwards of Ill. was a prominent personage in modern times. I have access to all his papers, & have in my possession at Rock Spring, correspondence of Col. Matthew Lyon of Ky. formerly of Vt. & famous in the Sedition law of 1798. I send you two Papers Baptist Records. One contains the operations of the Society I serve, recently. The other of April 2. contains a Memoir of Rev. Lewis Williams of Mo. He is a type of a class of "pioneer preachers" & in that sketch I am to illustrate those peculiar traits found in that class of men.

Where are you now to be found in or near Baltimore? Perhaps I may have occasion to visit that city, & if so will give you a call if you are to be there till Spring. I see you mention letters from Boon. Have you his autograph? Can you furnish me with one? If not, can you loan me one of his letters, if in his hand, & let me get an engraving — a facsimile of his autograph? Mr Sparks is very desirous of obtaining one. My address till May will be No. 31, North Sixth Street, Philadelphia.

Very respectfully yours
J. M. Peck.

[p. 3³]
Have you corresponded with Rev. Theo. S. Hinde, Mount Carmel, Ill.? He has trunks full of old documents.

[Postmark] Philadelphia Jan 25 Paid   PAID   ⑤

Dr. Lyman C. Draper
Baltimore, Md.
Jan. 25th. 1846.
Hist. Of the Mis. Valley
Memoir of Boone, &c

[p. 4]
Philadelphia, March 25th 1846

L. C. Draper, Dear Brother, Will you please write me by 1st May to <u>Rock Spring, Illinois</u>, an answer to the following inquiries concerning Col. <u>Daniel Boone</u>?

1. Number & names, & so far as you have it, dates of birth ages of his brothers & Sisters.

2. <u>Names</u> of his <u>Father</u> & <u>Mother</u>.

3. The substance of what you learned from Capt. Gass concerning Boone.

<u>J. M. Peck</u>

[p. 4¹]
J. M. Peck's Inquiries
Answered 6th May '46
L. C. Draper

[p. 5]
Rock Spring, Illinois Aug. 10th 1846

L. C. Draper, My dear Brother, I am in the very heart of old <u>Boone</u>, surrounded with all the published volumes, & many publick & private documents, letters, &c connected with his eventful history. I have succeeded much better than I feared in settling some doubtful & disputed points of his history. Your letter from Baltimore to this office of date May 6th has afforded essential aid.

I have not been able to obtain a single copy of Butler's History, <u>second</u> edition. Only 500 copies were printed & it is out of print. The Author who resides, & has an office as Magistrate in St. Louis has but a Single copy. I shall go there in a few days, & copy Boone's letter or official report of the battle of Boonesboro. I learn that the eldest daughter of Flanders Calaway (Mrs Jones) whom I knew 28 years ago, & several of the Bryan's line in Warren County Mo. near where Boone lived & died. Mrs Jones was the eldest daughter of Boone's daughter Jemima (afterwards Mrs Callaway) whom the Indians took prisoner.

From her & the neighbors I shall, no doubt gather many facts & incidents of that part of the old pioneer's life that belongs to Missouri. I have settled the question

[p. 5]
of his birth. It was in Feb'y 1735.

In 1766, Boone headed a party of hunters in East Tennessee. You will find this in Haywood's History of Tennessee page 32. He was on the waters of Cumberland river in Kentucky before 1769, when he went out with Finley & others.

Since I have been at home, I have had one week's attack of fever, have had sore and weak eyes for a month — and last week I had a daughter dangerously ill. She is now better — able to sit up.

We have some sickness, and the weather has been & still is very hot and dry. Early planted corn first rate — late planted much injured by the drouth.

Wheat, oats & hay good.

Yours Respectfully
J. M. Peck

[p. 6]
Rock Spring, Illinois, January 4th 1847

My dear friend, your very acceptable communication from Baltimore, of the 15th ult. came to hand in due season. My "Boone" was completed according to my engagement before the 1st Nov. & sent by mail to Boston. Perhaps I did not mention to you I wrote Boone by contract for Dr Sparks series of American Biography. It will form half a volume, or about 200 pps. I say inter nos, my compensation is one dollar per page. It is in press by Little & Brown, Boston, but the volume will not be out till April 1st. In respect to the execution of the work Dr. Sparks writes, (Nov. 20th) "I have read a large part of it, & I do think it remarkably well adapted to its object. It exhibits thorough research in ascertaining the incidents of Boone's life; and the Sketches of Western manners & the habits of backwoodsmen, which are interspersed, are well selected, drawn with Spirit, and add much to the interest & value of the work." Coming from that source, it will do. He gives more credit than I expected. When in Cincinnati did you see or hear of a table, or genalogical record of the Boone family, published by Mr Cist, & said to be obtained from the parish & family record in Berks Co. Pa.? That places Boone's birth in July, 1732 — whereas both your statement from Daniel Bryan & the family tradition make it early in 1735 — as I have given it.

The supposed Capture of Col. <u>Daniel</u> Boone by Col. Tarlton in Virginia, in 1781, is most certainly a <u>mistake</u>.* It must have been some other

*No, my friend, it is a truth, well substantiated. — L.C.D.

[p. 6¹]
for Daniel had "lots" of brothers & <u>cousins</u> — some settled in Maryland — others in Virginia, and some of their descendents are in South Carolina. I have detected &

repudiated a "right smart chance" of "humbug stories".

And so you came to St. Louis & did not call at my domicil!!! When at Vincennes you should have taken the stage direct to St. Louis which passes my door. You deserved to be sick for going a wild goose chase round by Terre Haute, at least 80 miles stage fare for nothing. You ought to have come to my house, & then I could have taken you to Fort Chartres, Kaskaskia or where Clark was, & on the route from Vincennes to Rock Spring the road for half the distance passes on Clark's old trace, especially about the Muddy & Little Wabash where they waded & suffered so much. There is no way you can retrieve this blunder in traveling but to come again & spend some time at my house. I have a room fitted up in style with more files of old newspapers, pamphlets, books, and manuscrips than you can find in six months traveling — nay, in <u>five years</u>. Now are you not sorry you did not come to the right place.

I send per mail, the paper in which is my Address "<u>The Conquest of Illinois</u>."

I have received several letters from Mr Ludwig with his books & am much obliged to you for giving him information of my Post office address. While at Cincinnati, did you hear any thing of Mr Perkins book on the North West?

[p. 6^2]

I have a proof sheet he sent me. His work will contain a vast amount of <u>facts</u>, well collated & sifted from errors & mistakes. It is out of press by this time. I wish you had sent your article in the Nat. Intelligencer to me, & I would have copied & sent it to Dr. Nowell. Can you get me a copy of the Intelligencer? I spent two days at his house in 1844, & he has been a frequent correspondent since. In Clark, you have the master Spirit of the west in military life. Boone had very little of the war spirit. He never liked to take life & always avoided it when he could. He is a type of the better class of our western pioneers; mild, gentle, humane, generous & hospitable to a fault — extremely cautious, and admirably qualified for the part he was destined to act.

I am now arranging all my books, papers &c in order, that I can refer to any one I please at a moment — preparitory to employing the pen. There is a probability — at least there is a correspondence on the subject — that I shall cooperate in the editorial department of the "Western Baptist Review," with My old colleague, Rev J. L. Waller. In that case I shall give "The Life & times of Vardeman" in a series of articles. Very probably I shall prepare Historical Sketches of all the religious sects in the Western Valley in two 8vo vols — while considerable time will be devoted to my "History of Illinois." Let me hear from you often.

Fraternally yours
J. M. Peck

Rock Spring Ill.   Paid 10.
Jany 4.

    Mr. Lyman C., Draper, esq.
    Baltimore, Maryland
Rev. J. M. Peck
Jan. 4th. 1847
Col. Boone's Memoir & character &c

[p. 7]
Rock Spring, Illinois Jany 3rd 1848.

My dear friend, your very acceptable letter of Nov. 29th has been on hand several days, waiting for convenient time for an answer. From all I learn, my life of

Boone is received very favorably. It is only but a few days since I have obtained a bound volume. The "Sheets" were sent by mail last Spring.

At the last anniversary of the "Illinois Literary & Historical Society," a resolution was adopted appointing a Committee (of which I was made chairman), to prepare against next anniversary a "History of Ill." Though the resolution was introduced without any conference with me, I understood its purport, as designed to push me forward in the work. My plan was an elaborate work, of labor & research, equal to two full-sized Octavo vols. but this move has put it into my head to write an epitomised History, after the style of Boone, leaving out all "documents," "laws" "letters" &c making a 12 mo volume of some 400 pp, and have it ready to report to the Society next July. My "contemplated work on the Religious sects of the Mississippi Valley," is still in contemplation. I have an application for a brief Sketch from Mr Perkins for a second edition of his "Annals."

I have Dr. Spaulding's History of Catholic Missions in Ky — Dr. Bishop's "life of David Rice" — "Bosser's Travels in La." and nearly every other currently published work except Capt. Pitman which Senator Breese from this state has. I have not yet obtained "Davidson's His. of Presn. Chh of Ky". I have seen and glanced a little into "Marette's History of the Valley of the Mississippi," but from hastily run-

[p. 7¹]

ning over its contents, am inclined to think it is made up with Documents & statements from others with very little discrimination. Mr. Butler of St. Louis states it is very erroneous & very defective. Very few persons who make the attempt have any idea of a <u>History</u>, or a <u>Biography</u>;

Proper History is a complete portraiture of the body politic, ... the whole world, the Church — the Jews, ... empire, nation, province, state, city, town, or family. All its parts, and at all periods of its existance, or for the period pretended to be given, should be set out in ... & Just proportions, with such extraneous events as have had influence of forming & moulding this body politic. A biography is the History of a Single person, with such connecting events as will explain & set forth his habits and character, like the back ground, light and Shade of a correct portrait. Were a professed anatomist to gather a mass of human fragments, out of due proportion, as a dozen legs, one arm, 3 or 4 heads, and mutila... portions of the trunk, put them together, and say "I have made a man," the unnatural & unsightly monster would resemble exactly at least three-fourths of our "Histories and Biographies." A historian & a biographer must have the genius of an artist; he must create, not a piece of fancy work but a real embodyment, a perfect appearance of the object he professes to deliniate. A state is a body politic, and a correct History of it, bears a perfect similitude to the portrait of an existing man. The same idea should be kept in view in biography.

My information of the "Girtys," was derived from

[p. 7²]

various sources. Mr Perkins has given Simon Girty a much better character than I could.

The manner in which Filson wrote his Sketch of Boone I had from the family. He read to the old man what he wrote who approved it as a whole. Substantially it is correct so far as it goes. The date of the Siege of Boonesborough was probably an error in copy.

I am well satisfied that the note from Dr. L. D. Boone (an acquaintance of mine,) is substantially correct about the feelings of Rivalship on the part of Col. Todd, at the disastrous battle of Blue Licks. I had full evidence from the uniform statements of Boone & Flanders Callaway & others, but I added the extract from Dr. Boone's letter as collateral proof. Such rivalries are natural, common, & characteristic of military men. The <u>Todd</u> family have disputed it, but their testimony is wholly <u>negative</u>, while the other is <u>positive</u>. De Monbrun, (a frenchman, who had a trading post previously at the "French Lick's" (now Nashville Ten.) was <u>appointed</u> Lieut. Gov. of Illinois by the Governor & Council of Virginia soon after the report of Clarke's Conquest was made & when the "County of Ill." was organized, which you will find in the Statutes of Va. Dec. 1778. He officiated for a time, it is supposed, for there are grants of land & other documents in the old office of Kaskaskia issued on his authority.

You can learn not a single thing from the <u>Hay</u>'s of this county. <u>John Hay</u>, son of <u>Major Hay</u> of whom you write was clerk of this county for more than 40 years, a very accurate man in business but full of blunders in historical matters. His father was an officer under Britain and resided at Detroit, & was with Hamilton at Vincennes; probably an Indian trader.

[p. 7³]
John Hay died some 3 or 4 years since. He was never communicative about his father and hence the notion amongst the people was that his father was hostile to liberal principles & American interests.

I have been & am still employed writing for several Newspapers: Sketches of Boone & other Pioneers for the Missouri Republican; a series of articles of the <u>History</u> of

Slavery in Ill. for the National Era at Washington. In Novm. I entered on the discharge of the duties of pastor of the Bap. Chh. in Bellville; preach twice on Sabbath & give a lecture on Historical & other matters Saturday night. Let me hear from you frequently, and especially if you find any spot in Clark's campain that needs clearing up. Yours afect'ly,   J. M. Peck

Rock Spring Ill Free J. M. Peck P.M.
Jany 3.
    Mr. Lyman C. Draper
    Baltimore, Maryland

[p. 8]
Rock Spring Ill. Oct. 10th 1848.
    L. C. Draper esq. Dear Brother, Your very interesting & acceptable communication of Aug. 22nd has lain on my table several weeks unanswered.
    I found out & traced up the mistake about Col. Todd in Boone from Judge David Todd of Missouri, whose post office address I could not learn while writing Boone. From the same source I learned that Col. John Todd was, in fact Lieut. Governor (a special office created by the Legislature of Va.) of Illinois when he was killed. He had been to Kaskaska, organized the new government, issued grants for land and a "proclamation," a copy of which may be found in Dillon's Historical Notes of Indiana, page 186. You may get a look at the Christian Review (Baptist) at the Baptist Publication office No. 31, North Sixth Street & in September No. you will find an article "The Grave of Daniel Boone", & two literary notices, Perkins' Annals, & Davidson's His. Of Presn. Church in Ky, which you should possess by all means. It was published by Carter of N. York.

Call on my successor, Rev. Thomas S. Malcom at the Publication office, make yourself known as a baptist brother, and a Correspondent of mine. You may there find large files of old Minutes of Associations, especially the Philadelphia association in the olden time, containing much curious historical matter.

[p. 8¹]

The only thing I have done in historical research for five months past is preparing an oration which I delivered to the Alumni of Georgetown College Ky. by invitation, and subsequently to the Alumni of McKendree College in Lebanon Ill. on the "Elements of Western Character". In this I attempt to trace from the remote sources, the peculiarities of character, of the puritans of the north, the Cavaliers of the South, the German, Irish, French, Welsh &c which in this Great Central Valley are in process of fusion & forming an amalgam. At both Colleges I had unanimous votes & heavy calls for publication, but I prefer to let it lie awhile, pursue my investigations further, and bring it out hereafter in a more perfect form. I may work out an article for the Christian Review from it.

I can give you no special information about the father of John Hay, more than you find in Clark's papers, Dillon & public Documents. I expect he was of no great account.

I have not yet gotten hold of Hildreth's work, nor Howe's Ohio; Shall obtain the former soon. I have not written any thing for the Republican since last spring. The number you got I think is the last.

[p. 8²]
I wrote a series of numbers on the early American His-

tory of Illions for the Illinois Journal of Springfield, have but a single file. If I can get a file, or even a partial one when I visit Springfield next winter, I will do it. They have no spare file in the Republican office St. Louis, but you would find no additional <u>facts</u> than you find in my Boone.

After getting my crops secured, I shall shut myself up and labor in my workshop during winter on my Illinois History — Vardeman &.c.

I was much obliged to you for the Literary World & your article on Virginia History. Let me hear from you frequently.

Yours respectfully

J. M. Peck

[p. 8³]
Rock Spring Ill. <u>Free</u> J. M. Peck P.M.
Oct. 16

Mr. Lyman C. Draper
Philadelphia, Pa.

[p. 9]
Rock Spring, Ill. July 29, 1850

L. C. Draper, Dear Sir, Yours of the 13th which arrived during my absence, has been read with great satisfaction. My "apology" for not writing to you for many months past is the fact that I knew not where to reach you, or most certainly you would have had no small trouble from me. If you go to Philadelphia, call at the Amer. Sun. School Union Buildings, 146, Chemist Street, enquire for Rev. Dr. Babcock, and if you find him, ask him to show you a <u>Book</u> called "<u>Annals of the West</u>," and you will learn what I have been about the past year. You will see I have revised wholly Perkins work, made it into chapters, with headings, left out various documents & put in matter, enough with the "appendix" to make 808 pps.

You will find in that much <u>original</u> matter pertaining to Ill. and Mo. never before published.

I have no copies but a few I purchased at <u>retail</u> price ($3.00) of Mr. Albach the proprietor; but I will endeavor to get you

[p. 9¹]

a copy to transmit by some private conveyance & advise you accordingly; but I desire you should see and examine the only copy to be found in Phia. which I furnished Dr. B. <u>You</u> know something of the labor to destroy the <u>fictions</u> & <u>traditions</u> of Western and all other History, in order to get in the truth. Mr. Perkins last Sept. wrote me an urgent request that I would revise & correct his part of the work, and sent me "notes" and your corrections, as you will see in <u>notes</u> pp. 77-101 & 171. Mr. Albach, the publisher, sells <u>all</u> his books as a Colporteur at retail. The edition (second) 3,500 copies for which he got more than 2000 subscribers. There are divers typographical errors which I could not make the boys correct. Besides this work, which made me work <u>hard</u> from Dec. 15 to May 15. I supplied the pulpit of the Second Bap. Chh now filled by Dr J. B. Jeter, from January to October 1849; was at my post amongst the sick, dying and dead; was at the Great fire, and amidst all the calamities the church paid a meeting house debt of $12,000. The

[p. 9²]

baptistes now have the largest & best constructed protestant house in St. Louis and stand No. <u>One</u> in public esteem. $1500 per annum for 3 years have been provided to employ 2 first rate missionaries to build up two other churches in the city at once. Providentially we have now a church of Germans & Hollanders, 3 ordained preachers & about 60 members. About 40 have been baptised the last year. We have the "German Mission Society for the Mississippi Valley," the Board of whh is at St. Louis, & we have 6 missionaries and Colporteurs at work in this field.

For a few weeks I am supplying the church in the absence of Dr. Jeters. The sabbath eve. following the death of the President, I had a sermon ready, it being announced in the paper, & preached it to a very large congregation; much to the surprise of the other clergy who did not wake up and get their eyes open until the following sabbath when they all followed suit. I have no idea of visiting Philadelphia — perhaps never. Your MS. vols. are certainly a vast treasure of historical & Biographical lore, & will be of immense service to the future historian. I have a very

[p. 9³]
large collection of Newspaper scraps & printed documents.

I have projected a work on the plan of the "Annals," to contain the "Religious Progress of this Valley." It is intended to contain the principal facts and occurrences of every sect from the first to 1850 with footnotes as in the "Annals," for references to authorities and for further details. It will include sketches of all the Colleges & Seminaries, missions, ... operations, Sab. School efforts, Bible Societies, Colporteur works &c. I lay out three years for the labor. First year: go over, collate, arrange, and make indices & notes on all my materials. This method will show me what is wanting. Second year, by correspondence and traveling fill up what is lacking.

<u>Third</u> year <u>write</u> out the whole for the press. It will make a book of 800 pps. size of the "Annals".

I have several smaller works to prepare in the mean time, one is a 50 cent book on the "<u>Germans & German Missions</u>", in which I shall develope some curious and startling facts. Please call on my venerable friend Rev. H. G. Jones, present my affectionate regards, & read such extracts from this letter as may interest him.

Yours &c.
<u>J. M. Peck</u>

[p. 9⁴]

<u>Postscript</u>, July 29

I find I have not half answered your letter. <u>John Russell esq. of Bluffdale</u> Ill. returned from Louisiana last April where he had been at the head of a Seminary for 8 or 9 years. He is now in a School in Carrollton Ill, where a letter will reach him for six weeks to come. I was with him at the commencement of Shurtleff College Upper Alton, last week, in fine health and spirited. He was appointed to a vacant post in that institution the day after he left, by a unanimous vote. Whether he will accept I cannot now say, but think he will. I am Editor of the <u>Western Watchman</u>, & have been since January 1849 — of which I send you a number or two — and if you can afford to pay postage on it will send you a file of this volume.

You must not put <u>great</u> confidence In <u>Indian traditions</u>. Their memories are like other peoples, defective, and they have many romantic "Legends," the production of fancy story telling & made without a single fact; such was the Mammoth Story

[p. 9⁵]

narrated by Jefferson about the "Big Mammoth." The
more I examine Indian history the more fiction I discover.
"Drakes Lives of the Indians" has much fiction. His story
about Black Hawk and the Black Hawk War are Slanders
on the people of Illinois — a few grains of truth in a
bushel of chaff. You will find the facts in the Appendix
to my "Annals."

I have fished out some details about Col. Clark, not
published. He was frequently in St. Louis in 1779, when
at Cahokia — very intimate in the family of Gov. Leiba
— and it was expected he would marry the Governors
Sister. It was that year he found out the British & Indians
were projecting an attack on St. Louis, and made his
proposition to the Governor to aid in its defence. His
conduct at Vincennes concerning the projected invasion
of New Orleans, and with the French minister Genet
broke him down with Washington's administration &
sent him into the shades.

Let me hear from you again soon. I have just resigned my postmastership. It plagues me too much. Letters will reach me here still.

Yours fraternally
J. M. Peck

[p. 10]
Rock Spring, Ill. Sept. 17, 1850.

My dear friend & Brother, Your very acceptable letter of Aug. 28, arrived here when I was in bed, too sick to
read it. Since I became convalescent & able to sit up I
have read it with much interest.

I started to attend the General Assn. of Baptists in
Missouri, in Boone Co. on the 15th August. On the 20th,

having reached the Settlement, was taken sick — disease congestion of the liver, an old enemy — that usually attacks me on the fatigue & exposure of traveling; became convalescent; had a relapse & reached home sick & broken down Sept. 5th. I am now able to sit up & write a little, but feeble and gather strength very slow.

The principal thing deserving notice, is your statement that you have documentary evidence that Col. Clark did relieve St. Louis in 1780 (May). Do you find any letters or Journals in Clarks handwriting that says this? The MS. papers of the late Auguste Chouteau (& he was an intelligent and very correct man & a friend to <u>Clark</u>)

[p. 10¹]

say no such thing.   And certainly Clark was below the mouth of the Ohio establishing Fort Jefferson before May 1780, and from thence with two men went on foot through the cane brakes, swamps & swam the high waters to Harrodsburgh Ky in <u>June</u>.   Here he persuaded the officers to close the land office, raised a force & was over the Ohio in the Indian country in August 1780.   Clark left Kaskaskia, as near as I can ascertain, the last of February with a party in boats for the position below the Ohio. His command in Illinois had been superceded by the appointment of Col. John Todd, who came to Kaskaskia in 1779.

Besides how could Clark relieve St. Louis when actually invaded? The Story is he appeared with his men on the <u>bank of the river opposite St. Louis</u>. But at that time, this spot was a wilderness: not a house & <u>no ferry</u>. The ferry was from Cakokia, below a large heavily timbered Island (now gone) across to the present site of the U.S. Arsenal <u>three</u> miles below what was then St.

Louis. The <u>fact</u> is, the Indians had been decieved by the british, and instead of fighting Spaniards or Mexicans, as they were made to believe, they found they were fighting their former friends — french traders — and in parties drew off. Expresses had been sent by Chouteau and others to Ste. Genevieve for relief, and a party of men came from there, <u>after the fracas was over</u>. Another <u>Fact</u> is that Leyba, the Governor, was a traitor, very likely bought with British gold, & did all he could to prevent the people fighting as they did. Immediately after the enemy dispersed the Chouteaus and others sent off a deputation to New Orleans to impeach the Governor Leyba of treason to the Governor General; and in one month he died suddenly — tradition says by poison from his own hand.

Nicollet's report is a tissue of blunders. He got his stories from Old Pierre Choteau, a thick-headed old Frenchman, whose memory could not be trusted, and who knew very little.

My "<u>History of Illinois</u>" is worked up in the "Annals". I shall have occasion soon to send a small box of books to the Bap. Publication Society in Philadelphia, & then will send

you a copy of the "Annals". You cannot get it in Cincinnati.

I have never seen the "2 vols. Olden Time Magazine" of Pittsburgh. Where, or from whom can I get it? My projected "Life & Times of Vardeman" remains <u>Statu quo</u>.

I am about negotiating the sale of my farm & possessions at Rock Spring. If I succeed shall buy or build a small, quiet, retired dwelling near the College Upper Alton, have a garden & fruit yard, and devote the remnant of my days to carrying out my literary projects.

Let me hear from you occasionally. This office will be changed to <u>Shiloh</u> P.O.& removed 2½ miles the 1st day of October, by my arrangement. Address me to <u>Shiloh</u> P.O. St. Clair County Ill. until further notice.

Yours fraternally,
J. M. Peck

[p. 11]
Rock Spring, (Shiloh P.O.) Illinois
March 20, 1851

Lyman C. Draper esq. Dear Sir, Your very acceptable letter of January 16, arrived at my desk while absent to Springfield Ill. While there I was taken sick, and did not get home until the first of this month, and since I have been unable to bring up "lee-way" in my correspondence. I am still unable to leave my house, have a bronchial affection, amongst other infirmaties; my voice has become impaired, and I have not been able to preach since January. The honest truth is I am an old, worn out, broken down man, and there is no use in denying it. Hence I have done very little in my literary projects for many months.

While absent, the oldest church now in existance in Illinois (Bethel 8 miles N.W. from Rock Spring) elected me the pastor for the year. Though I have written and urged them to make an effort to get some one else, they

[p. 11¹]
are still waiting for me to get well. Last fall I left two copies of the "Annals" in Belleville for Col. Bissell, & Col. R. M. Young Clerk of the H. of R. Subsequently Col. Bissell called on me as he started and I furnished

him two more copies. After this I saw the man in whose care I left the copies in Belleville and the Stupid Jackass had sent the Books by mail to Washington City. Col. B. returned to Springfield where I saw him, & told him of the mistake and requested him, (if the Books got safe in mail & without expense) that I would direct them to be sent to Philadelphia. He returned to Washington late in the session but I have not yet heard about the books. If this mode fails, I shall continue to make a copy reach you before many months.

Your speculations about Clark appearing "opposite St. Louis" in May, 1780, at the time of the attack are most certainly fabulous. As to any dependence on conver-

[p. 11²]

sations with Genl. Clark in St. Louis they are no better than the ... and traditions that have floated around. William Clark, Governor of Missouri Territory knew no more on the subject than the traditions of others. And as these traditions, with the statements of those who were living in 1780, have been proved by the records of the church to have been sheer mistakes, so are these traditions. Nicollet in his public document has made egregious mistakes. He calls the Governor Lebas, and imagines him to have been a Frenchman, whereas he was a Spaniard, and his name Leyba. Nicollet got his news from Old Pierre Choteau, who died in 1849, and Choteau (Pierre) was as stupid a Frenchman as I wish to converse with in 1818. All he ever knew was about a little Indian trade. His brother Auguste was a man of reliable information & left some Journals & papers. Clark never appeared on the bank of the river "opposite St. Louis," as this old tradition is, for opposite St. Louis was a wilderness, a thicket, no path, no intercourse. The intercourse from Louisiana was below the arsenal opposite Cahokia.

[p. 11³]
It may be that the people at Cahokia sent an express to Clark at Fort Jefferson in April, 1780 as you say you have the "message" but I am confident Clark never went back there in May. You are aware he was superceded in the command in Illinois by the appointment of Col. John Todd. He Todd arrived in Illinois early in 1779, (say May) organized the government, was what Virginia called "County Lieutenant." He had command of both the civil and military Departments, and his powers of office were the same as formerly were exercised by the Deputy Commandants under the French Government Very extensive. (See his Proclamation in Dillon's Indiana, i. p. 186.) Clark remained under Todd through 1779, & had charge principally of the Indian Department. His station was at Cahokia, & he had frequent intercourse with St. Louis, lounged about there many days at a time, was an intimate visitor in the Family of Gov. Leyba, had a period of flirtation (courtship) with the Governer's sister; and the old folks used to say in St. Louis, promised to marry her. At least she got quite bewitched, and after

[p. 11⁴]
Clark left the country, and her brother, Leyba, died, as he did (some said he took poison) in a few weeks after his traitorous conduct in the attack, she retired to a convent. These facts I have from Colonel John O'Fallon of St. Louis, who was nephew, and the "pet child" of Col. Clark, and heard him tell "the oft repeated tale" of his adventures in St. Louis in '79. It was that season, through French traders and friendly Indians, Clark got the

intelligence of the projected attack on St. Louis, which was to have been that autumn, and <u>he</u> in his visits to St. Louis gave Leyba warning, and offered his services with volunteers from Cahokia, Kaskaskia &c. Leyba gave no credit to these warnings, politely declined all aid, affirmed the Indians were peacable, & that this rumor of an attack was deserved no credit. His behavior previous and at the time of the attack, fixed the impression on the minds of the people on both sides of the river that he was a traitor, and designed to have the place surrendered to the British.

[p. 11⁵]
Immediately after the Indians a few British retired, the Chouteau's and other leading French inhabitants dispatched a barge with an Express to New Orleans, with an impeachment, or an account of his traitorous conduct in the attack. He shut himself up, would see no one, & died as I have mentioned.

In the absence of all written evidence from Clark, I maintain he was not at Cahokia or St. Louis in May 1780. At that season, when the waters were unusually high, it would have taken him from 12 to 15 days to have come to Cahokia by water, and by land it was impassable; the rivers, sloughs and lakes being more than full. It was a season of extreme high water. Then what use for <u>him</u> to return. Commandant Leyba the preceding year had declined his service and discredited his report of the intended expedition. He had been ordered by the authority of Virginia to establish Fort Jefferson. He had no troops — no command whatever in Illinois. He never would have disobeyed orders by going on an expedition out of the Jurisdiction of Virginia. You may rely on it that all these stories amongst Clark's men about his appearing opposite or in St. Louis with an army, originated in his interviews & his communications to Leyba in 1779. And in most of the stories and traditions 1779 is the year in which the attack is placed. The true date Mr. Primm was enabled to fix beyond all controversy (May 26, 1780) from the register of the church, in which the names of the Slain, the day of the attack, and the funerals of each are given.

The flirtation business with the Spanish Senorita will furnish you a little episode in a life so exclusively military as that of Col. Clark. I regret I cannot yet give you her name, and will yet if I can find it. The old soldier used to chuckle over it, as no small interlude in his adventures, though he never admitted he intended to marry her.

Please let me know from time to time how you succeed in your collections, and whether you are near the press in any thing. I suppose you read the Christian Chronicle. In the one for Feb. 26 is a letter of mine

from which you may learn the progress and prospects of Illinois.

You will see mention made of a Sermon preached at the call of the Legislature. It has just been printed in St. Louis, and you will receive a copy in a few days, which please let my old friend Rev. H. G. Jones read, & present my kind regards to him.

Sincerely yours
J. M. Peck.

Rock Spring, (Shiloh P.O.) Ill. August 14, 1851.

Lyman C. Draper esq. Dear Sir, Yours of May 9th has been a long time on hand waiting for an answer. For more than six weeks I have been variously afflicted. I have had a succession of large boils, the rheumatism at the same time in my knees, especially the latter half of the night & and fore part of the day, and I have been obliged to avoid all writing that could be dispensed with. During one week I had an attack of Dysentery, a disease, which with sporadic cases of a modiform of cholera, have prevailed throughout the country to a limited extent. Yet it has not been a sickly season, and now health prevails. St. Louis has less sickness and fewer deaths than is usual in large cities.

Our College proceedings you have seen in the Chronicle. The annual meeting of the "Literary & Historical Society of Illinois," occurred at the Same time, but finding it a poor chance to attend to such matters in due order we have changed the anniversary to the last week in November, (Wednesday) to be held in Alton City, and have two or three days devoted to lectures, discussions & conversations. You could not do better than to be here at that time & spend the winter at my house, and examine all my files of papers, old

pamphlets, magazines, manuscripts and all sorts of documents, live on corn bread, and the luxuries of our soil, and get rid of dispepsia, and every   ill flesh is heir to".

A committee has been appointed to investigate and make report on certain documents said to have been discovered in the archieve of the diocese of Quebec, concerning the early French Jesuit, and other Catholic missions in Illinois. A document has been published in the "Shepherd of the Valley," the Catholic paper in St. Louis and which is edited by the archbishop, ... which the names of missionaries in <u>Illinois</u> ... labors are given, from 1653, & for more than one hundred years after. Now every document and amongst these, the "Lettres Edifiantes," from the Jesuites, all give <u>Marquette</u> in 1673, ... the first missionary amongst the Indians in the Illinois country, and we suspect these Quebec documents, are forgeries or antedated. I suspect they were written about 1760, or '70, and partly from "tradition."

Now can you throw any light on this subject? Have you any thing in your collection that prove or disprove the Quebec statement? Please communicate.

Recently I wrote an article of some 25 or 30 pp. print for our <u>Christian Review</u> now published by Colley & Ballard, New York. It is on the

[p. 12²]

"<u>Annexation of Louisiana</u>." I give a historical sketch of the province & its changes, but go somewhat into detail in the circumstances of its purchase by the United States, was an act of Providence. You are aware, I presume, that Mr Jefferson, or his cabinet, nor the Amer. Congress never projected the purchase of Louisiana, and when it was done by Messrs Livingston and Monroe in Paris, and the news reached Washington, it came on the President & Cabinet, like a terrific thunder in a clear sky. They desired, & sent out Mr. Monroe for the purpose, to purchase the Island of Orleans, and thus secure the port of New Orleans, & the navigation of the Mississippi, which you know had been a matter of negociation for twenty years. Have you <u>Marbois</u> History of Louisiana, & specially of this treaty? He was the negociater on the part of Napoleon. If you have not, look about the antiquarian book stalls, & stores in Philadelphia, & you may find one. It was published by Carey & Lea in 1830, only a year after Marbois in French appeared in Paris.

I have been some time & shall continue to be for some time yet writing "Historical Sketches" in the Missouri Republican. These are regularly transferred to the "Western Watchman," now edited by Rev. William Crowell, and published

[p. 12³]
by Messrs Crowell & Brower, who is a Phidelphian and formerly was on the committee of the Publication Society. If you can spare conveniently $2 for the paper I would recommend you to have it, for these and other historical matters. I would pay & send you myself but am hard run at present for cash. I can get (I think) the back Nos. containing these sketches if you commence with vol. 4 which began with July. I have written Skitches of the early settlements in "Boone's Lick," Mo. which never before appeared in print.

Your soldier at Cahokia, in 1780, mistook that year for 1779, as many others have done. Clark certainly was not at Cahokia in 1780. He left Kaskaskia in February, 1780, for the post below the Ohio, & never returned to Illinois. Gov. Ford's History is not published. Gen. Shields our Senator in Congress has the MS. and Ford left a dying request he would publish it but he is in doubt. From his M.S. the articles have appeared in the papers. It is both defective & erroneous. Gen. S. will be at my house soon and I am to examine & advise. Judge Breese has no history of Illinois in hand.

John Russell is teaching a Seminary in Carrollton Ill.

and would be much gratified to receive a letter from you. Write soon.

Yours fraternally,   J. M. Peck.

[p. 13]
Rock Spring (Shiloh P.O.) Illinois, March 27, 1852.
L. C. Draper,

My dear brother, Yours of Jan. 23, has been suffered to lie on my table unanswered until this time, which you may regard as a just penalty for not calling on me last fall. If you had come to my house, my wife would have nursed and fed you, & I could have cured you of the dyspepsia & every other ill that flesh is heir to. You could then have had a warm room, plenty of corn bread, beef & bacon, and overhauled all my books, newspapers, pamphlets, journals, &c for "Pioneer History," and gone off in the spring a much sounder and wiser man.

Besides, you would have seen me laboring on a new work, quite unexpectedly: "The Mississippi River Illustrated" from its extreme source to the gulph of Mexico. Two publishing houses, one in London, the other in New York have projected a rather splendid work of that sort, of which they expect to circulate in Europe & the United States some 15,000 or 20,000 copies in large quarto size, with about 50 fine engravings on Steel, to illustrate various views along the river. The work will first appear as a sereal, in numbers, each No. containing four plates & from 12 to 16 pp letter press in quarto. One of the publishers, an intelligent German literateur, is in St. Louis, and the first I heard of it, I had been recommended to him to provide the letter-press. I am now on No 4., between Lake Pepin and Prairie du Chein, progressing downward. My business is to provide the letter press for each number, at the rate of about one in each month. I have to describe

the natural & physical character of the country; Scen...; its natural history, animal, mineral & vegitable; the manners, customs, legends &c of each class of people — Indians, French, English, Americans; historical sketches; hunters, trappers, voyageurs, bonrieur de bois, traders, backwoodsmen; progressive improvemnts, towns, cities, water craft, commerce &c. &c. Such is the general character of the work. On the 11th inst, I sent T. S. Anthur, for the "Home Gazette," a legend of the "Maiden's Rock," at Lake Pepin, very much improved (I think) on all former sketches of that story, done up in true Indian style. This work will take all my spare time for this year, as it requires thorough investigation & care. The Indian legends are intended to be what "Indian traditions" really are. They are like the novels "founded on fact," but the "fact" is the very smallest part of the concern. But the rest of the work is correct. It requires labor in a more extensive sense than I first expected.

I thankfully received Mr Mayers Discourse on Col. Cresap, Logan &c & examined it with much interest. I have not seen De Hass His. of West. Va. or heard of it except in your letter. Some years since I corresponded with him, or rather he began it, but I have lost his P.O. & know not where to write. I must have his work. Have you got a copy of my "Annals" yet? I ordered one to be sent from Washington city, which was sent there by mistake, & I have another reserved for you here if that has failed; but living as I do in the country, I find out no private conveyance till it is too late. I have obtained nothing further

[p. 13²]
of the Mission Documents of Quebec. The November meeting of the Ill. Historical Society was a complete failure. Of three committee men to provide for it, one was absent, another sick, & a third did nothing. I could not attend. Indeed, I cannot travel about as I once could. I have been writing some sketches for the Chris. Watch. & Reflector, Boston; an recently sent on the first part of "Father Clark," the first man who preached the gospel west of the Mississippi, in "Spanish times." I have but a single file of the paper in which my "Sketches" of Boone's Lick &c came out, or I would send you some.

If some publisher would get out <u>Vardeman</u> and give me the customary perquisite, I could readily write his "Life & Times," but having spent a vast amount of time in the vigor of my life, in writing for the benefit of others, I am now compelled in old age to write where I can get the perquisite, to pay some debts & meet current expenses. I <u>hope</u> yet to live to complete my project of a work to include the religious, literary & benevolent Annals of this Valley.

Hon. <u>John Reynolds</u> of Belleville, Ill. ex Governor, ex Congressman &c has in press "<u>The Pioneer History of Illinois</u>," from the earliest French visits to the organization of the State Government, in 1818. Much of the materials for the early History he gets from My "Annals". He came here, in 1801, has a good memory for <u>dates, events</u>, & <u>names</u>, and will patch up a useful book, in duodecimo, some 300 or 400 pp.

[p. 13³]
The past week, I have written for him some 27 cap pp. M.S. of the <u>moral & religious pioneers, churches</u>, &c. I will obtain and preserve you a copy. My article, written

by his urgent request, will be a separate chapter, with my name appended. Gov. Ford's M.S. history (a very imperfect concern) is in the hands of Gen. Shields, Senator in Congress, but I advised him last summer not to publish it. It is very imperfect, has many stale anecdotes and coarse jokes conserning some of our public men that are apocryphal, and would do no credit to Ford's memory. Our peaches were all killed by the severe winter in December & January and a thaw between. On two occasions, for eight days it never thawed in my vicinity in the most protected, southern exposure. On Monday morning, January 19, the thermometer in the country 18 degrees below zero. In the warm atmostphere of St. Louis 15°. In Iowa & northern Illinois 20°.

Yours fraternally

J. M. Peck

P.S. I send you some documents.

[p. 13⁴]

Rock Spring (Lebanon P.O.) Illinois, Dec. 10th 1852

L. C. Draper esq. My dear friend: Yours from Wisconsin, of the 11th ult. reached me a few days since, and had I not received it, before this time I should have sent the "Annals" & also the "Pioneer History of Illinois" to Leverington, Pa. Both are sent this mail, & I hope you will receive them in due time & order. You will find the "Pioneer History" a unique thing, quite characteristic of the writer. The "Pioneer History" is a curiosity, a kind of historical Salmagundi, some mistakes of the author, but many more of the printer. The "Governor," as we call him, (for so he was at the time of the "Blank war") bought an old pannage press & fonnt of type, and employed a Journeyman printer, who knew nothing of proof-reading and but little of printing. Gov. Reynolds is more correct in dates, names and events than most of the pioneers, but he has made some mistakes. I intend to have one of his books bound with interleaf, and correct carefully his errors with notes, for the future historian.

The "Annals" have some typographical errors, which you will readily detect.

You enquire about my professional and literary engagements. I am still pastor of Bethel church, but have given notice of declination on first January, in hopes they will obtain another pastor & leave me at Liberty. I may continue longer on a temporary supply until they can obtain & settle a pastor. In addition

[p. 14]
to writing for the "Christian Review," the "Christian Repository" at Louisville, and several other periodicals, for the customary perquisite, my principle labor for 12 months has been the "Mississippi River Illustrated," of which I gave you a Sketch last spring. It has been in course of publication in Europe for some months in quarto numbers. I sent off the No. Viii, a short time since which included the Section from Burlington to the mouth of the Missouri. The issue in New York will commence early in January. The engravings progress slowly & I can keep ahead of the press. With Nauvoo, I have given a truthful picture of Mormonism, and near Alton at the Piasaw rock I have made a new version of the Piasaw story or legend, which I obtained from Go-sah, an Ot-tah-wah Indian, and quite intelligent & educated. (By the way that should be the orthography of Ottawa some broad & highly aspirate.)

Perhaps you have seen in the papers the terrible calamity by fire on my presses, and the destruction of a large part of my valuable library & newspaper & periodical gatherings for 40 years. It was the building known as "Rock Spring Seminary," about 150 yards from my dwelling house. In the upper story, which contained four rooms, was my library, & all my files of papers & pamphlets amounting to 8000 or 10,000 volumes, the most unbound & packed in boxes or on shelves. I was fitting up the lower story to make a family residence that

[p. 14¹]
I might sell my property & improvements on the public road. During the past season at convenient times I have the roof & siding all renewed with new door and window frames, and my son was putting in new doors & windows the morning of Nov. 18; the wind strong and cold severe from the northwest. He had a small fire in the fireplace, and protected as he thought from all harm. While absent a few moments a spark was blown by the wind (as it seems) among some shavings and door & window casings, for the windows & doors being open. The north chamber which was the windward side was fitted up with shelves for my bound volumes — a room 16 by 20 feet, & shelves, all filled. My two sons at home threw from this room most of the books out at the windows, before the flames drove them out, but some 200 or 300 volumes were burnt on the ground, near the building. I have lost nearly all my files of my own periodicals, for 20 years, which I doubt if ever they can be replaced. I had the reports and other documents of all the philanthropic and benevolent societies in the U.S. and some in England, which are nearly all gone; more than 40 volumes Niles Register unbound; all Duff Green's Telegraph and other papers; Congressional Globes, Public documents from the administration of Mr Monroe, State documents from early times, and as auctioneers advertise, many things

"too numerous to mention". I am not left entirely destitute

[p. 14²]
for I had several cases & shelves in my dwelling house where I kept, Minutes of Associations, pamphlets of various kinds, books I had occasion to use in my business, & all my journals, Correspondence, and manuscripts. These were Safe. I have what some would call an ample library yet. But old files of newspapers & pamphlets, and other periodicals are gone that I think a duplicate cannot be found on earth. I doubt if it is possible to make up a file of my own publications. I have hopes yet, if the <u>Good One</u> spares my life and health for four or five years, completing my most important work, "<u>The Moral Progress of the Mississippi Valley</u>," but I must now go abroad for a portion of my materials, whereas before this fire I had a supply. I must visit & copy from the archives of all the missionary, Bible, Sunday school, and other societies that have operated in this Valley, which will require a year's labor.

My plan now is to visit the Atlantic States in the Spring and see what I can gather up there. Strong expressions of sympathy comes in every mail. My loss is a public one, for I intended all these for a public library. My pecuniary loss is not less than $5000. I had a small insurance of $700 on building and property. That you may not think me hopelessly destitute in literature I find it will require a building 16 by 20 feet, ... 10 feet story with shelves around to furnish room for what I still have. Mind & not make the mistake many have about the <u>Daniel Boon</u> (not Boone) for there were half a dozen. Get <u>the</u> Daniel Boon. Please write often.

Yours fraternally, <u>J. M. Peck</u>

My suggestion of "the Daniel Boon," is to put you on your guard. Mr Cist of Cincinnati gave the pedigree & relatives of a Daniel Boon, but he got the wrong one, and singular it may appear, the family had nearly all the same first names with the Daniel's family. They were cousins. The Boon connection was much larger than supposed, and so many of the name of Daniel, Squire, Samuel &c it is not strange that Daniel Boon was born at two places in Pennsylvania, in Maryland & in Virginia. J. M. P. (over

For the Christian Chronicle.
LETTER FROM DR. J. M. PECK.
Rockspring (Lebanon P.O.) Ill.,
November 19th, 1852.

Messrs. Editors: You will probably notice in the papers that the building, known as "Rock Spring Seminary," was consumed by fire on yesterday morning, between nine and ten o'clock. With it went a large part of my valuable library, and what is worse for future generations, several thousand volumes of newspapers, periodicals and pamphlets, in unbound files, the gatherings of forty years, and the editorial exchanges, all of which I preserved carefully. The building, which had become my property by purchase, had the upper rooms fitted up for my library and as a depository of my collections. The roof and sides had been recently re-covered, and my son was repairing the lower story, by putting in new doors and windows, &c., for my family residence. The wind was strong, and he had been absent but a few minutes, and on return found the fire so far kindled in some shavings and door trimmings several feet from the fire place, as it could not be extinguished. My two sons mounted the second story through a window, and threw out the books from the shelves until the fire drove them out. Some hundreds were burnt on the ground where they fell; the flame becoming too violent to enable us to remove them. The loss in value cannot be less than $5000; insurance, $700. My journals and other manuscripts, my letter correspondence for forty years, such volumes as I was using, with some late files of papers, (of which the *Chronicle* was one.) Minutes of associations and other materials for the religious history of this Valley, were at my dwelling house and saved.

Will you please give notice to my correspondents, that hereafter my post office address is *Lebanon*, St. Clair Co., Ill. The post office at *Shiloh* is defunct, and no *material* there to make a new post master.

Yours fraternally,   J. M. PECK.

[p. 15[1]]

You will find my story in life of Daniel M. Spark's Biography correct, except the story about Col. Todd &c p. 119. That story I found since the publication was reported by McGary & his friends, to screen <u>him</u>. There was no rivalship in the case. Col. Todd at that time was County Lieut. of Illinois. See "Annals," p. 697, 698, & 699.   [P o s t - mark] Carrollton, Ill.

Extract of a letter from the Rev. John M. Peck, one of the Baptist Missionaries at St. Louis.

"It has been denied by historians that the aborigines of North America ever offered human sacrifices; but that the Pawnee do, is now past all doubt. They worship the planet Venus, which, in their language, they call "the great star," and to secure the favor of which, they offer human sacrifices. These are generally prisoners taken in war. There is now in St. Louis a Spanish boy, about 10 years of age, whom they took prisoner last year, and were about to offer him. He was ransomed by Mr. Lisa, a citizen in this town, and trader amongst them, who brought him to this place. Some time ago this sanguinary band took a Pado woman prisoner, and devoted her to the sacrifice. As she was pregnant, the diabolical rite was put off till after her delivery. As soon as she recovered from child-birth, she stole a horse and made her escape. Being obliged to leave her babe in the hands of these bloody idolators, it was immediately transfixed to a shani pole, and in this situation offered to their god.

[*Hartford Times.*] [Nov. 1818]

[p. 16]
Rock Spring (Shiloh P.O.) Ill. April 4th 1853.

L. C. Draper esq. Dear Brother, Yours of the 17th ult. came in due season. I have been writing a few articles for the Mo. Republican of St. Louis, on the "Explorations of the Mississippi Valley," and given some new facts and corrected some errors and mistakes. One fact is that Cabeza da Vaca, mentioned by Shea, p. X., who was with Pamphilius de Narvaez, ("Annals" p. 26) was shipwrecked on the coast of Florida, 1528; & with 3 Spaniards & a negro servant, was made prisoner by Indians, and after wandering from one nation to another, actually crossed the continent to the Colerado, & down towards Acapulco. He & his men crossed the Mississippi a dozen years before de Soto. Friar Marc in that remote Spanish settlement within 25 miles of the Pacific, with the negro for a guide, set out with an expedition into the interior of N. America, took the walled town of Cibola, were on the waters of the Gila, describe the mud towns of the Aztecs, came on the great plains east of the Rocky mountains, at the very time the expedition under de Soto were on the Mississippi.

Another fact is that for 30 years before Marquette & Joliet made their voyage of discovery, the French missionaries & traders had learned from the Indians the character & course of the Mississippi, & the tribes on the borders; and Marquette had learnt their languages, &.c. The romance of this expedition has turned to a grave matter of fast business. I have traced their expedition minutely & accurately. A third fact is, there was a large Indian town

[p. 16¹]
on the Illinois river between La Salle & Ottawa of 6000 or 7000, and that there was the first French settlement in Illinois, as early as 1678, and it was called Kaskaskia. Our modern Kaskaskia was made 12 years after, down South. Marquette was succeeded by F. Allonez, at the northern Kaskaskia. Prof. Shea's new work throws much light on these early explorations. Have you seen it?

Hon. Mann Butler of St. Louis is writing the History of the Ohio Valley, taking the whole sweep of country drained by its waters. It is a revision and enlargement of his history of Kentucky.

I am arranging to start east on the 19th inst. My address until July wil be care of Rev. L. Colby, Publisher, 122, Nassau Street, New York."

I have put our Philadelphia folks up to organize a sort of General Baptist Historical Society, as a department or appendage of the Publication Society, & they will do it at the anniversary May 4th & 5th, and have called on me for an address on the occasion.

Can I do anything for you while east? Write me as above directed.

Yours as Ever. J. M. Peck.

[p. 16²]
Rock Spring (Shiloh P.O.) Illinois, Sept. 16, 1853.

My dear Friend: How do you get along with old Boone? Don't keep up the interminable blunders of his pedigree & family. I see recently, a document has been presented to the Historical Society in Pa, in which his birth place is <u>Berks</u> county. The writer has gott on the wrong family just as Mr. Cist did. The Boone family were quite numerous at the birth of <u>our</u> Daniel, & were in 3 or 4 branches, & what makes so many mistakes, the names of Squire, <u>Daniel</u>, & George, were in each. The document to which I refer, gives the authority of Episcopal church records in Berks county. This I investigated in 1846, and found it was another family. It makes Daniel's birth in 1735, when the Daniel of that family was born, but <u>our Daniel</u> was certainly born in 1732. Boone told me himself he was born in that year, but could not recollect the month but thought it was <u>Feburary.</u> (See my <u>Life of Boone</u> pp. 11-13.)

I have found some evidence since that leads me to think his birth was later possibly in July. There were very probably more Boones than "George and Mary" that migrated from England early in the 18th century. This is another fact that has been overlooked. One settled in Maryland, another in Virginia &c. I am now confident Daniel, <u>our Daniel</u> had uncles in the country, & "lots" of cousins, among whom were one or more Daniels, Squires &c. Our Daniel's father was certainly Quakerish, if not a quaker. Others of the family remained Episcopalians.

I have just received a letter from John Warren Hunt

[p. 16³]

Esq. of your City. He has published a Gazetteer of Wisconsin. I write to him by the mail that carries this letter.

Gov. John Reynolds has made inquiries of <u>me</u> for the information you need of him. So has my old friend & parishioner Robert Lemen. I have encouraged both to write you, but they can give you no information behind mine. In the "American Pioneer" you will find my articles of Capt. Joseph Ogle & of the attack on Fort Henry. His descendents in this country know nothing personally, and the old man never boasted of his exploits. I gained the information from his compeers who are now all gone.

In my late tour I was successful in reclaiming some of my losses. I obtained copies of the Reports & Periodicals of the various Benevolent Societies.

While gathering & arranging materials for my "Moral Progress," I am preparing a series of small books for Sunday School libraries, family reading &c which I call "Pioneer Books." They will be from 150 to 200 pps, 18mo. One I am now on is "The Indian Captive," or "John Tanner" among the Chippewas. The next will be "Father Clark, or the Pioneer Preacher." I shall also prepare the "Life & Times of J. Vardeman.".

The Indian Captive is for the Bap. Pubn. Society, "Father Clark" for Heath & Graves, Boston of the ... Sun. School Union. I have work enough for the men laid out.

Yours sincerely   J. M. Peck

J. M. Peck
Sept. 16, '53

[p. 17]

CIRCULAR

For many years the undersigned has been engaged in collecting books, pamphlets, newspapers, reports of philanthropic societies of a general and denominational character, for a library. His main object has been to obtain materials of every kind to aid in developing the history and characteristics of the central portion of the United States lying on the waters of the Mississippi.

A calamitous fire on the 18th November, 1852, destroyed the building containing a large portion of his collections, with a part of his valuable library of choice books.

This whole property, which cost him several thousand dollars, was intended to become the property of one of our public Institutions, at a central point, where it might be kept together and accessible to the public for future time.

At the urgent solicitation of many friends, whose opinions he felt bound to respect, for several years he has been preparing a work for the press, the plan and design of which may be indicated by the following title:

THE MORAL PROGRESS OF THE MISSISSIPPI VALLEY.

Such a work, after much condensation, and using statistical tables, would be comprised in an octavo volume of about eight hundred pages. The general plan would be a combination of annals, and continuous history of periods. It would aim to give, from authentic documents and the testimony of living witnesses, a concise account of the principal facts concerning the rise, progress, and present condition of each Christian denomination, from the earliest settlement to the present time — the commencement and progress of Sabbath School and Bible Class Instruction — Tract distribution — efforts of Bible Societies — the distribution of religious books by itinerant preachers, and latterly by the employment of colporteurs —the labors of missionaries, and the operations of the denominational missionary societies of the Atlantic States in this Valley; with the operations and effects of any other benevolent and philanthropic societies that have aided in the moral progress of the inhabitants. Education, and its progressive effects by common schools, public schools in cities, academies, seminaries and colleges, will be reviewed. The Press, with its various influence and bearings, will be given. Laws in the several States for the conservation of morals and good order, with the influence of our political institutions on the morals of the people, will be noticed. Biographical Sketches of ministers of the gospel, jurists, legislators, and other laymen, who in public or private life have aided in the advancement of morals and religion in this Valley, will be interspersed through the work.

The undersigned had materials nearly or quite ample for such a work before the disaster by fire, and he finds that by effort and perseverance a large proportion of the necessary documents can be replaced.

With this view the writer has spent several months in travelling, principally in the Atlantic States, visiting the depositories of the various societies that at any period has had laborers in this field, and obtaining such aid as their archives could furnish.

CORRESPONDENCE SOLICITED.

But to do justice to every Christian sect, and make such a work accurate, and deserving confidence as a correct portraiture of the past and the present, the author needs the aid of individuals and public bodies in the field of his labor.

For the present, he is desirous of knowing where he can obtain in pamphlet or any other form, the proceedings of the various ecclesiastical bodies in this Valley; as synods, presbyteries, conferences, associations, conventions, &c., catalogues of colleges and seminaries, and the proceedings of all other literary institutions, with the documents of *every kind of society* professedly of a moral or philanthropic character in this Valley, are wanted. Catalogues and other publications, with letters from officers of the colleges of the Mississippi Valley, previous to 1840, the writer has in possession; but he needs the necessary information of the new institutions, and the progress of the old ones, since that period. He specially solicits the correspondence of gentlemen who may feel an interest in the projected work, and be willing to aid in furnishing facts.

It will not be the business of the author of such a work to hold controversy, or presume to adjudge disputes between religious sects, but to give the facts as accurately as possible, and leave the reader to deduce his own inferences, and do his own moralizing. The author proposes to allow a wide margin for diversities of opinions on disputed points of faith and practice; but it will be his province to judge of the legitimate tendencies of customs, institutions, and social organizations, whether as a whole they have been beneficial or injurious to the moral progress of the population of this Valley.

The author expects to have this work ready for the press in three years, should his life and health be spared, before which, arrangements will be made with some enterprising publishing house, who will give it a wide circulation at a reasonable price. The undersigned will have no responsibility in its publication and sale, and hence no person need address him on that subject, unless a responsible publisher or bookseller.

J. M. PECK.

Rockspring, Ill., July 20, 1853.

N.B. — *All letters and other communications should be sent to Shiloh Post-office, St. Clair County, Ill.*

[p. 17¹]

Can you furnish me any documents from any of the Religious & philanthropic Societies in Wisconsin? Can you name any ministers or clerks with their post offices who keep the records of any or all the ecclesiastical Sects?

J. M. P.

[p. 18]
Letters from John M. Peck

Covington, Ky. Dec. 28, 1853

L. C. Draper esq. Dear Brother: Yours of Nov. 27, was in my P.O. box on my arrival in this city the 17th inst. I am now most comfortably situated in one of the rooms of the College Edifice erected for the "Western Bap. Theo. Institute." The "Institute" has been divided & ruined by two factions — one so "doggedly conscientious," that they would not cooperate with Slave holders in any form, the other blustering about "rights of the south." Yet these factions are now as loving as brothers need to be in view of dividing the spoils. In this project their consciences work together most amiably. But just as they had amicably agreed to apply to the legislature for a division of the spoils between Fairmount & "Georgetown" a third party starts up, & claims a voice in the matter, until a Convention of the denomination throughout this Valley can

[p. 18¹]
act on the whole subject. Gov. Morehead, who lives in Covington, has a remonstrance on the subject, strong & full, to meet the application for a division. I do not expect we can resuscitate the Theological School here, but

the Covington people have <u>rights</u> in the case and a further compromise will be necessary. The property here has been invoiced recently, as other like property sells at $350,000 — leaving over $300,000 after all debts & claims are satisfied.

If Fairmount gets $100,000; Georgetown, or wherever the South Western Baptists locate, gets $100,000; the other share including the buildings will make a <u>Female</u> Bap. College for all time to come.

Gov. Morehead will obtain for me the Document, containing Clarks life, journeys &c prepared by himself at the

[p. 18²]
solicitation of Mr. Jefferson. Gov. M. also has a <u>Report</u> drawn up by himself & Chapman Johnson for the U. S. Supreme Court in a great land suit about the Western end of Ky. many years since. Their clients had to send over to England & obtain copies of all the treaties with Indians in the South West, before the revolution, with maps &c. This he says is indispensable to the history of those times, & he thinks it throws light on Boone's travels in Ky. and also on Clark's position below the mouth of the Ohio in 1780. I shall have the document in a few days & if I find any thing for you will write again.

"<u>Life of Vardeman</u>" — soon as I can finish "Father Clark," & the "Indian Captive", I shall work on the "<u>Life & Times of Vardeman</u>." Moore, Anderson & Co. have proposed to publish it. I can have it ready in 6 months or less.

[p. 18³]
I must look at your project of <u>Chh Library</u>, soon as I can obtain the document you mention. Send on the Minutes

of your Convention.

My prospects are encouraging here, though the church has been in a low state a long time.

I thank you for the names sent as Correspondents.

Prof. Drury & family are well. He presides over the "High School" gotten up by the city authorities.

This is a pleasant and delightful city for a residence; quiet & social, worth a dozen Cincinnati's with its "swinish" propensities.

Please get the enclosed into the possession of Rev. Mr. Delany.

> Yours fraternally,
> J. M. Peck

[p. 19]
Covington, Ky. April 10th 1854.
L. C. Draper esq. Cor. Sec. State Historical Society &c.

Dear Brother, Yours of March 4th announcing that your Historical Society had elected me an "Honorary Member," was received in due time. Please present my kind acknowledgments to your Executive Committee, and assure them I will do what I can to promote their object. Hereafter my whole time will be devoted to preparing the works for the press, I have so long projected.

In a week or less I bid a final leave to this city, & return to Rock Spring, Ill. where I shall remain at home the remainder of my days.

Hence please remember that hereafter my P.O. address is Shiloh, St. Clair Co. Illinois.

In addition to the works on hand of which I informed you last year, I have two more thrown on me, that I cannot avoid making. One is a Memoir of my old friend & ministering brother Elder J. B. Meachum, who fell dead while preaching in his church, 19th February. Meachum was a very extrordinary man, for one of his color & with the disad-

[p. 19¹]
vantages of his Situation. He was about my age & had been trained first in the Sunday School, & then in the ministry under my supervision. In a Section chapter or Appendix I purpose discrying the question of giving moral and religious instruction to slaves, and how this should be done.

The other book is a Sketch, or sort of memoir of Elder Joshua Bradly, now living at St. Paul, Min. over 80. I make this to help him in his infirmity & poverty. He has been a real pioneer among the Baptists. Have you ever seen him?

I am now visiting Cincinnati daily when the weather is good, & making notes & extracts from old files of papers in the Methodist Book Concern for my "Moral Progress of the Mississippi Valley." To day I have overhauled & gotten the cream from Bishop McKendree for a Sketch of his life & labors.

You have seen probably in the "Christian Times," and perhaps other papers, my resignation, & the reasons. Hereafter I expect to confine myself exclusively to the pen.

Fraternally yours, J. M. Peck

[p. 20]
Rock Spring (Shiloh P.O.) Ill. May 15th 1854.

L. C. Draper esq. Dear Brother: Your letter of the 8th came this morning to my table.

In my "Boone" pages 44-45, you will see in a note, an extract from Hall's "Sketches," suggesting the fact that the Boone's were employed by Henderson & Co. to find how the "land lay". At that time it was doubtful & I left it where Judge Hall did. Since, further investigations have convinced me of its truth. It is an important key (if true) to unlock the life & character of Boone. Let us leave it out and see the result as follows.

1. You have D. Boone, wandering in the wilderness of Ky. two whole years, without end or aim — for he made very little by hunting but kept on <u>exploring</u>.

2. You have Henderson & Co. buying a vast tract of Country of the Indians at Watauga, perfectly ignorant of its quality, how the rivers run, its boundaries &c. They paid £10,000 in goods, & yet knew nothing what they purchased. Shrewd speculators would have employed a competent & <u>confidential</u> agent first to examine the country.

3. You have <u>Squire Boone</u>, coming out with supplies & finding his brother in the wilderness, without end or aim.

[p. 20¹]

4. You have Daniel Boone at the treaty of Wautaga, a very important personage, and Henderson & Co. & still no object — no reason for it.

5. You have him <u>publicly</u> employed as the prime agent, removing to Ky, opening a road & building the fort at Boonesboro'. Now reverse the circumstances & see how natural & consistent the whole appears.

1. It was indispensible to success that all the preliminary steps to the purchase should be kept secret, and a confidential agent employed to explore the country. Other individuals & companies were rivals & looking westward for wild lands. Boone was the <u>very</u> man for such a mission, a perfect backwoodsman a good hunter, and could be relied on for secrecy.

2. Henderson & Co. knew what they were about when they purchased, & had Boone at Watauga to guide them in making their boundaries.

3. His brother Squire was fitted out with supplies & knew what he was about & was equally trustworthy.

4. I have had it from a dozen sources, from the family & others, that he was often questioned as to his <u>object</u> in spending two years in the wilderness of Kentucky, & he always evaded a direct answer. Boone had that sense of honor, not to say conscientiousness that when

[p. 20²]

he had solemnly pledged himself to secrecy, he could not be made to divulge it. After the whole affair was ended, the purchase declared illegal & the tract in the Green river country given as a remuneration to Henderson & Co., others who were in the secret, hesitated not to speak of Boone as having been employed. But Boone himself always evaded a direct answer on that point.

Some 4 or 5 years since I saw a gentleman from Tennessee, a relative by descent of Henderson (a nephew I think) who told me he had seen amongst the old papers letters &<u> instructions</u> to Boone about this first exploration, and assured me I need no longer doubt about Boone being their confidential agent.

I wrote a series of numbers, by contract, on Boone in the Missouri Republican in 1847, after my book came from press, in which I gave this view of the case more definitely; but the file went to ashes in my fire.

Judge Butler must have misunderstood me about Boone being a <u>partner</u> in the Company. I do not understand it so. He was employed as a confidential agent to explore the country, and very likely, if the title had been good he would have had a tract of land.

On page 119, is an error in my "Boone", about Col. Todd, from Dr. L. D. Boone's correspondence of Chicago. I learned subsequently that this

[p. 20³]
story was told by McGary & his friends. Col. John Todd was then Lieut. Governor of the <u>county of Illinois</u>, with his commission in his pocket, but being Senior Colonel in the Kentucky militia, & on his way from Williamsburgh, Va. to the Illinois country, took command in the Blue Licks massacre, & fell. See my "Annals" pp. 697-698. He had been to Williamsburgh on matters pertaining to the Illinois country.

Probably you have seen in the "Christian Times" in February what perports to be a "Documentary History of Shurtleff College." It is anything else but <u>facts</u>. Poor old Mr Loomis, in his dotage & memory gone, was induced to put his name to these articles, by a man for designing purposes. While at Covington I had application for "records" in my possession, to make a counter & full statement. Shurtleff College called first, Alton Seminary, had its origin at <u>Rock Spring in</u> 1827, and, by advice of the late Dr. Going Lathers, was removed to Upper Alton. In July, 1831, Going, Dr. Edwards & myself selected the site & made arrangements to purchas 122 acres of land. In March 1832, I went to Kaskaskia & engaged the old man Loomis to remove to Upper Alton & open a school while the first building was erecting.

In 1836, he resigned all connection with the Institution, cut up some <u>queer</u> capers, left the Baptists & joined the presbyterians, & was an enemy to the College 15 years. I expect a pamphlet will be published.

Yours &.c.   <u>J. M. Peck.</u>

[p. 21]
Rock Spring (<u>Shiloh</u> P.O.) Ill. July 3rd 1854.

L. C. Draper, esq. Dear Brother, Your letter of the 8th May has been answered. I now enclose you a Scrap about Boone which is going the rounds of the papers. I wrote it for the Alton Telegraph, & it is now going from paper to paper without any concern of mine. The writers of Boone have made an unsocial, moody misanthrope, with no social affections, because they found him two years absent from his family, roaming over Kentucky without aim or end. He was not such an idle old fool as to roam about the woods without object. <u>Entire ignorance</u> of Boone's character & of his being a confidential agent of Henderson have caused this great & ridiculous mistake. I may have sent you a similar Slip before but have forgotton. Gov. Reynolds is engaged in writing "Sketches" of his Journeyings from Belleville, Alton, Chicago, Buffaloe to N. York & the Crystal Palace a year since & back by the Ohio river. It is full of statistics & facts. John Russell of Bluffdale is at my house & has been preparing an address to the "Philosophian & Literary Society" of McKendree College on Wednesday at Commencement. I am writing a sketch of J. Vardeman for Rev. Dr. Sprague of Albany N. Y. for his great work on the Amer. Pulpit. I have been two months overhauling and arranging my Minutes of Associations

[p. 21¹]
and all other pamphlets of this Valley, that I can now lay my hands on what I want. "Clark," the "Indian Captive" and Rev. J. B. Meachum will have to be thro' the press before the fall trade.

Yours fraternally, <u>J. M. Peck.</u>

Rock Spring, Ill. (<u>Shiloh</u> P.O.) Oct. 17th 1854.

L. C. Draper Esq   With this letter I send you a part of my article on the late Rev. J. Vardeman, copied from the Chris. Repository, of Louisville Ky.   Remainder in next paper.   You will see I have given you due credit for the notes you took from Morgan Vardeman & sent me a dozen years since.

I am nearly through with "<u>Father Clark</u>," & the most of it has gone to press.   Sheldon Lamport & Co. Nassau Street New York are the publishers, as they will be of all my "<u>Pioneer Books</u>."   Have you received Gov. Reynolds new book of "Sketches" &c?   He told me some time since he should send you a copy.

My health has continued good since Spring; no illness of any kind, but I have to follow up the plan of avoiding fatigue and exposure.   Occasionally I preach when the weather is favorable; but in no case more than once per day.

Tomorrow & next day is the agricultural Fair of this county, near Belleville.   The committee have gotten my name announced for the "<u>Address</u>" without my knowledge or consent, but I have published my declinature, and as they have gotton no one else they will have to go without a regular speech.   If you get the Christian Review, you will see a historical

article on the presbyterians of West Pennsylvania.   That is another specimen of my "<u>Moral Progress</u>."   Do you get the Amer. Bap. Memorial from Philadelphia?   In the Oct. No. is a sketch of John Leland.

We have had the longest & severest drought I ever knew.   South of Rock Island & Ottawa, there is not over half an ordinary crop of corn. In the middle and eastern section of the State, many a farmer has not made an ear. The very abundant <u>mast</u>, will fatten pork for home use, & winter the pigs.

Much of my time has been occupied with business affairs. I have built me a little house, & it required personal supervision.

Will you make your arrangements to attend the general Anniversaries at Chicago next May, that I may meet you once more?

Let me hear from you soon & often as convenient.

Yours fraternally   <u>J. M. Peck.</u>

[p. 23]
Rock Spring (<u>O'Fallon Depot</u> P.O.) Ill. Jan. 12, 1855

L. C. Draper, esq. Dear Brother, I wrote you Oct. 17th & sent you a paper containing a sketch of Vardeman, but have not heard from you since. Have you received the <u>second</u> paper, containing the rest of Vardeman?

I think I have mentioned before, my mistake in <u>Boone</u>, pp. 119-120, about Col. Todd being unwilling to wait for Col. Logan. I gave Dr. L. D. Boone of Chicago as authority, but I found out the mistake in 1847-8. McGary wrote a letter some time after the battle at the Blue Licks, to Col. G. R. Clark, to exonerate himself from charges, & that letter with McGary's statements to persons produced the wrong impression. Col. John Todd was Lieut Col. in Fayette County. Col. Benn. Logan the same in Lincoln, & Col. Floyd in Jefferson, each equal in authority in their respective counties, but Col. Todd would have been senior or chief commander in his own county. There was no rivalry but the closest friendship between him & Logan. Then it is a fact affirmed by Levi

Todd & other officers who survived the battle that Col. John Todd, Col. Boone, Lieut. Levi Todd, & every field officer, & many who held

[p. 23¹]
inferior command held a consultation, on the bank of Licking, and <u>unanimously</u> resolved to wait for Logan & his party to arrive. McGary was a man of terrible passions, entirely reckless & unprincipled & became furiously mad when he found the officers were resolved to wait, & rushed into the Licking, & called to everyone who was not a d--d. coward to follow him. He & he alone caused the dreadful disaster of that day. I learned this from Hon. David Todd of Missouri, Doct. John Todd of Springfield Ill. both Sons of Lieut. Levi Todd, who had often heard their father state this, & that he wrote it in his Journal. This Journal he loaned to Gen. Joseph H. Daviess in 1811, & could not find it after Daviess death. I have other authorities for this correction.

In p. 159 of my "Boone," you will find "His beautiful farm near Boonesborough" &c. It should have read: "His beautiful farm at <u>Boone's Station</u> near Lexington, &c. Boone made a "station" & a farm a little S.E. from Lexington a few miles, & he & Col. <u>Levi Todd</u>, lived neighbors for many years. Boone lost other tracts in law, but this was his "<u>Farm</u>."

p. 191: I give the names &c of Boone's children, & mention <u>Jesse Boone</u> his fourth

[p. 23²]
son. It should be <u>Jesse B. Boone</u>. He was elected a member of the first Legislature under the state Government in 1820, was taken sick and died in the City Hotel, St. Louis, where he boarded, while the Legislature was in

session. Have not the date but think it was in Septbr.

Have you discovered how often the old pioneers make mistakes in dates, & confound incidents? I cannot trust one of them without going behind them, and testing them by State papers, legislative Journals, and other correct documents. Old Gov. Reynolds of Belleville, with whom I am quite intimate, has about as correct a memory as any one I have known, and yet I am constantly detecting him & setting him right. And, by the way, have you seen his "Sketches" in a little 12mo volume? He told me he would send you a copy by mail. He thinks you are a great man & I have not yet undeceived him. He is now writing his own Life & times. He calls it "My Own Times." It will be full of gossip.

I have lately received an 8mo volume published by Lippincott, Grambo & Co. Phia. lettered "The Old Red Stone Presbytery", a capital antiquarian book of the Scotch-Irish Presbyterians of Western Pennsylvania. I have written a Review of the work for the St. Louis

[p. 23³]
Presbyterian, of which Rev. Dr. Rice, late of Cincinnati is editor. I will send you a copy soon as I receive it. Just at present my mails & post office facilities are all deranged. The great eastern mail is carried on the Ohio & Mississippi Rail Road to Salem Ill. where the stages take it. "O'Fallon Depot" is 2¼ miles from my house by the highway, though the rail road runs just ⅔rd a mile north of me & the office at Shiloh has been changed to "O'Fallon Depot" to day. This will throw my papers & communications into disorder for a month, before I can get all my papers, periodicals & letters rightly directed. But I shall have a permanent, daily mail each way, when it once gets regulated.

My "Father Clark," I suppose is published, but I have not seen it. I am now preparing "The Indian Captive," to be out before April. I have just received by mail "The Life of McCurdy" one of the old presbyterian Ministers of Western Pennsylvania with an "Appendix" containing in short sketches the outlines of 35 other ministers in that quarter, all dead. Let me hear from you soon as convenient. Yours fraternally,

J. M. Peck

P.S. My health has not been good since Nov. 10th — a series of colds. My wife is ill also.

[p. 24]
Rock Spring (O'Fallon Depot P.O.) Illinois
June 5th 1855

L. C. Draper, Cor. Sec'y. of the State Historical Society, Wisconsin.

Dear Sir, The "First Annual Report," of your Society, you had the kindness to send me came to my office last week. I send you in return by mail (postage paid) by this mail, my "Father Clark, or the Pioneer Preacher." A few typographical errors I have corrected in pencil marks. My health has been very defective since November, & early in April, I was attacked severely by my old enemy, Congestion of liver. It is only about two weeks since I have been able to get out from home, and yet I have but little vigor. My long illness has stopped my book-making, and articles for periodicals & reviews. My next Pioneer volume, will be "Incidents of Pioneer Life," made up of several biographical articles, Sketches &c. The aberation of Rev. James Tanner to the Unitarians & his erratic course, will render it expedient to pospone my "Indian Captive" until, the public mind is quieted down by that event.

When is your <u>Boone</u> to go to press? Unless you get it out soon, I may send out mine, made up from the articles I wrote for the Mo. Republican in 1847-'48. It is a series of Sketches of Kentucky Pioneers, principally Boone & his companions, in a familiar style for boys & girls to read. I suppose it will not come directly in competition with yours, with its "<u>Illustrations</u>."

Your "Society" with the aid of $500 from the State makes noble progress, & its "First Annual Report" & appendages, is no mean document. In glancing over its pages, I find some mistakes, as is common especially with every man writing from memory some years after events occur.

And, I suppose by this time you have found out that the memories of <u>old men & women</u> cannot be relied on for particulars. They almost uniformly confound two or more events together in their memories.

One way to correct their narratives is to refer constantly to the documents published in the time or soon after the occurrence

of the events. Sometimes you get contradictory statements from different persons, and it requires long & patient investigation to get the truth.

The "Early Times" by H. A. Tenny, p. 94, contains many errors about the Black Hawk war.

The "Indian Nomenclature" by Mr. Calkins, & customs of the Chippewas, have a number of errors. Hon. H. R. Schoolcraft is the only authority I admit in the sounds & meanings of Chippewa words. No one should write on such subjects <u>now</u> without careful examination of the Great National work on the Indins gotton out under his editorial supervision. I refer to the Imperial Quarto volumes or "Parts," as they are called, & entitled "Historical & Statistical Information respecting the history, condition and prospects of the Indian Tribes of the United States; collected and prepared under the direction of the Bureau of Indian Affairs, per Act of Congress March 3, 1847." This great work is being published by Lippencott Grambo & Co. in Phia. I do not see this work mentioned in your collections. I am under the impression that copies

[p. 24³]
are distributed gratis to State Libraries & State Historical Societies. Five volumes or "Parts" have been issued, and I think a "Sixth," was reported by the Editor as ready for the Press last winter. You ought to have this work, if you have nothing else.. It is the test by which you may try all such articles as those to which I have referred as being erroneous. I will add that Rev. Mr Bronson's articles (p. 110) on Indian names, is very defective. Mr B's knowledge of Chippewa must be very superficial. Dr. Edwin James edited "Tanner's Narrative" (The Indian Captive) which I have, & he made a translation of the New Testament into that Language which has been proved very incorrect. His vocabularies, Songs &c in Tanner, Mr Schoolcraft informs me, & this is confirmed by others, are very incorrect. I suggest you correspond with Mr Schoolcraft, Washington City, "Indian Bureau," & you can learn how you can get his great work.

Yours fraternally,
J. M. Peck

P.S. Do not expose my free criticisms to the parties interested, for no man likes to be exposed.

[p. 25]
Rock Spring, O'Fallon Depot P.O., Ill. Dec. 3rd 1856.

L. C. Draper, Esq

My dear Brother: Your consoling letter on the decease of my wife of the 24th ult was received in due time. I knew nothing of the injury to your "right hand" you mention & wondered that with the vigor of health & in the midst of active life, you did not <u>write</u> more. Occasional newspapers, containing the monthly proceedings of your Board, have been read with interest, & a month or so past I was greeted with your second volume of "Transactions." I should have furnished you some thing in my line of business, but, alas! I am an old, worn out, broken down servant. I cannot do as much with my pen now in <u>one week</u>; as I could do 6 and 7 years by-gone in 24 hours. If you get access to the Christian Review for October, you may see its leading article on "Campbellism," which, probably is the last elaborate article I shall undertake. For 7 or 8 months I have been failing in <u>flesh</u> as well as other complications of disease. At the time of my wife's death, I was a mere skeleton, and my strength & vigor failed as fast as <u>atrophy</u> increased. My phician used tonics, Stimulating bitters, and other remedies to no purpose. On election day he examined me, & recommended the disuse of all further <u>medicine</u> and try <u>Regimen</u>, & suggested Old London bottled porter & animal Jelly.

[p. 25^1]
Another old physician, on consultation urged <u>Cod-Liver, Oil</u>. I have used these articles three times a day for four weeks, and the change in my whole system is surprising. I have gained 50 percent in physical Strength, & begin to gain flesh. I could not have survived two months. Cod-

liver Oil is an efficacious article to aid digestion and restore a vitiated system.

I have had to relinquish all my plans & projects of books — Pioneer Books, Moral Progress of the Mississippi Valley &.c. I shall leave in Manuscript & in collations of print, a large supply of materials. If I so far recover strength & health as to be enabled to do <u>two</u> things, it is as much as I expect. 1st. I have to arrange the books in my library, & a large stock of Newspapers, & pamphlet literature, put labels on them, & prepare them to be disposed of as my <u>Will</u> directs. Two principal divisions are destined one to the Library of Shurtleff College; the other to the St. Louis Mercantile Library association. 2nd. By the urgent solicitation of many friends I have commenced a series of "<u>Reminiscences</u>" to cover over more than 60 years. Much of this will appear in Newspaper columns, & eventually worked up & appear as a <u>post-humous</u> work. Rev. Dr. Babcock of Patterson, N. J. will be my literary Executor. All my manuscripts, Journals, kept for more than 40 years, Correspondence &c will be deposited in a Case, for which I have made provision in the St. Louis Mercantile Library Association. Let me hear from you when convenient.

Yours fraternally   <u>J. M. Peck</u>

[p. 26]

Rock Spring, O'Fallon Depot P.O. Ill. May 26, 1857

L. C. Draper, esq. My dear friend: Your well known chirography, appeared this morning on the envelope of a printed circular, at O'Fallon Depot P.O. while I was waiting for my mail. Very much obliged to you for it & hope you will yet be successful in bringing out some of the old pioneers. I have received occasionally newspapers containing notices of your "Proceedings" in the Board of your society. I am still wearing out; going down the hill every year, and cannot get up again. From 1st February to the last of March I was unable to go out; had three successive attacks of my old enemy congestion of liver. Since then I have gained slowly, by using daily Old London Porter & Cod-liver-Oil. Without the constant use of these articles of regimen I have a rapid tendency to atrophy, & in consequence to great prostration & feebleness.

Some of my friends & physicians are trying to persuade me to spend the hot months of July and August in the <u>north</u> — up the Mississippi, to Wisconsin, Minnesota, &c. I have serious doubts of ability to stand the fatigue of Journeying, but it may invigorate me. All will depend of increasing vigor, weather &c

Will you please inform me if there is a rail road in operation from Madison to some point on the Mississippi & what point? I think you have a regular traveling line of Cars from Madison to Milwaukee, or Chicago, or both. If you have no rail road to the Mississippi,

[p. 26¹]

what is the mode of travel, & is it by day or by night? If I attempt such a tour it must be in a mode the least fatiguing. Would it not be a "surprise," if I should enter your "den" some day in summer?

I ordered the <u>Christian Repository</u>, edited and published by Rev. S. H. Ford Louisville, Ky to be sent to you for your Historical Society. Do you receive it? I ordered the <u>Illinois Journal</u> to be sent as in that paper I am publishing various biographical articles of Old pioneers. Being unable to get out pioneer books as I intended, I have turned my attention to writing "Sketches," "Reminiscences," &c and publishing them in various newspapers and other periodicals where they will be accessable to future historians. I suppose you have seen and examined the new periodical, "<u>Historical Magazine</u>." Is not that exactly the thing?

I am fraternallly yours

<u>J. M. Peck</u>

[p. 27]

Rock Spring, O'Fallon Depot P.O. Ill.

July 10th 1857.

L. C. Draper esq. Dear Brother, Yours of June 15th came to hand in due time. I am obliged to you for the information of the Rail road from Prairie du Chien to Madison. It is just the thing. My tour is now marked out. I go on a steamer up the Mississippi, to Smith's ferry, opposite the mouth of Galena river, where my children live, spend a week there, then take the boat from Galena to Prairie du Chien, thence to Madison. I intend to leave here in about ten days, & reach the capital of Wisconsin by the 6th or 8th of August, so as to be there before the second sabbath.

You will do me a favor by finding me a plain, quiet boarding place for 8 or 10 days, & drop me a line to Galena. The abom-

[p. 27¹]

inably fashionable hotels are a nuisance to me, with all my infirmaties. I cannot endure a crowd.

I have a notion that you have a pure, elastic, bracing atmosphere at Madison, and that is what I need. One main purpose in my journeying, is to invigorate my worn out system & escape the debilitating heat of this region, and thus prepare myself to stand the coming winter.

As to want of time on your part, there are two things that can set that matter right.

1st. I shall not need your <u>time</u> to visit with me. I have done with sight-seeing, and cannot <u>walk</u> about, as I once could.

[p. 27²]

2nd. I can pay you double price in my labor for every hour you lose by my presence in Madison. Only put some of your rough material into my hands, and if you can do as much and as well in preparing it for the compositor, in a given number of hours, as I can with all my infirmities, then I will give up, & own myself beaten.

It will not detract from my health & comfort, & afford me pleasure if you will permit me to aid you for a few days.

I ordered the Ill. State Journal from Springfield to be sent you. Do you get it? I am making that paper one of my medicines to preserve such historical & biographical facts as should

[p. 27³]

be preserved for the future historian. I am now working out the "<u>Ogle family</u>." The patriarch, Capt. Joseph Ogle, was at the Siege of Fort Henry, (Wheeling). He emigrated, with his <u>three sons</u> & several daughters to the Illinois country in 1785. He lived for about 20 years within 3 miles of Rock Spring, though before I came to the state, & died there in 1821, in his 81st year.

Yours fraternally,
J. M. Peck.

[p. 28]

Rock Spring, O'Fallon Depot P.O. Illinois, Sept. 24, 1857

L. C. Draper: Dear Brother

I reached Chicago, at 1¼ ock P.M. the day I left you,

but met there the most abominable atmosphere <u>for my use,</u> to be found on the continent. It was raining, wind from N.E. blowing up the Lake, damp, chilly, "raw," and destructive to all safe breathing. Chicago in every respect is a <u>great humbug.</u> They are now building many hundreds of light, flashy, fancy buildings 5 and 6 stories high, all for show; nothing firm, strong or permanent about them, and on the most expensive <u>credit</u>

[p. 28^1]

system ever known or tried. Everything you see is deception, trick, humbug. For ten minutes on Sunday I saw the sun through clouds and mist. Monday at 4 ock PM. I entered the cars of the Southern Michigan Rail Road, & made a visit to my late Wife's Sister, & children, including a dozen students male & female, when I taught a Seminary in Duchess county, N. Y. 42 years bygone. Now they are old men and women — grandfathers and grandmothers. They live in Cass Co. Mich. I returned from Michigan to Chicago, by the Mich. Central Rail Road on the 25th Aug. and spent

[p. 28^2]

three days with the family with whom I boarded while at Covington, Ky. and who nursed me while sick. I again encountered the damp, rainy, chilly air, and Lake winds, from the effects of which I have not yet recovered.

Friday, Aug. 28: I took the Cars for Galena, where I spent Saturday & Sabbath and down to Smith's ferry on Monday, where I found my son Henry and another gentleman from St. Clair county. On Thursday morn in company with Mary E. Smith, my housekeeper I took the Cars at Galena Sandoval & home, leaving 4 others to take the night train & follow on. We reached Decatur & put up at a hotel & got a comfortable night's rest. Next morning at 7.40 the night

[p. 28³]
train came on and our Company. We reached Rock Spring, Friday night at 7 ock, and to all appearance well & vigorous. In two days I had a bilious attack, and in a few days it turned to a severe congestion of liver. A course of medicine and a sore mouth followed, and I am now as far back as I was last March. This traveling for health "is not what it is crack'd up to be."

I can only set up and write and read a little. It will be a month before I can be able to work.

We have great wheat crops. Our Farmers thresh out from 25 to 52 bushels first rate wheat per acre. From 35 to 40 bushels very common.

Yours truly <u>J. M. Peck</u>

[p. 29]
Letters from H. M. Peck

Rock Spring Ills. March 19th / 58
Lyman C. Draper   Dear Sir,

Your communication of the 14th reached the late residence of my venerable Father to day. But too late to reach him, as he had gone beyond the reach of worldly matters. As you will probably have learned before this reaches you, he departed this life at twenty minutes before nine oclock PM on the 13th of the present month.

You request him to copy some portions from his journals. If it would answer your purpose for me to make the extracts you refer to I would be hapy to do so.

[p. 29¹]
His correspondence Journals writings &c, are ultimatly to be placed in the Library of the St. Louis Mercantile Library Ass'n for reference, & probably you could get what you want from them then.

Anything I can do for you will be a pleasure.

Your humble servant
H. M. Peck

P.O. Address
O Fallon Ills.

[p. 30]
Rock Spring Ills. July 23d / 58
Lyman C. Draper   Dear Sir,

Yours of the 19th is before me together with your highly interesting article on "Moral & Religious Instruction." I have perused both with deep felt interest.

I have never seen a better article in defence of the Bible in Public Schools than the one I have just read.

Dr Babcock has all the Journals MSS. &c of my late lamented Father in his hands. Their ultimate destination is the "St. Louis Mercantile Library Association" Where they will remain for future reference.

[p. 30¹]
My late Fathers Library was principaly divided betwen Shurtleff College & the Mercantile Library by his Will. Each Vol had been designated before his death by having the name of the Society pasted within the cover. The remaining lot was sold at public sale by the Exector Geo. Trumbull Esq'r of Belleville. Haywood's Hist of Tenn. was among the latter class. I am under the impression that it was purchased by Ex Gov. Reynolds. If so I think I can procure it for you. Which would give me pleasure

to do so.

I would feel myself under obligations did I receive your Soc'ty publications.

Yours with Esteem,
H. M. Peck

[p. 31]

<u>Died</u> near the close of the year 1830, at Kaskaskia <u>Gen. John Edgar</u>, aged upwards of 90 years.

A Review of the Illinois Magazine, in Dr. J. M. Peck's "Western Pioneer", of March 16, 1831: "Illinois Monthly Magazine. We have just recieved and hastily perused the fifth no. of this valuable periodical. It contains the following articles: Intestate; Sketch of the life of Daniel Boone; On the use of Tobacco; Liverpool and Manchester Railway; Reminiscences of Pittsburg; Poetry, To a White Rose Bud; and The Consultation. The <u>Intestate</u> and the poetry, are original; the others are selected, but valuable articles. The Intestate is a fine tale, we

[p. 31[1]]

think, from the pen of the editor. The Sketch of Daniel Boon, appears to be abridged from Flint's work. We have noticed several inaccuracies, which may claim a passing notice at some future time. We say inaccuracies, for we have some sketches of these events taken from the account given verbally to us by Boon himself, with whom we spent several hours at different times, listening with delightful interest at the reminiscences of his eventful life.

"The time of his death is incorrect. He died in 1820, at the house of his son-in-law, Flanders Calloway, Charrette, Montgomery County, Mo. where he had made his

[p. 31²]
home for many years.

"We differ altogether in opinion from Mr. Flint, that "he appeared to us the same Daniel Boon, if one may use the expresson, <u>jerked and dried</u> to high preservation, that we had figured as the wanderer in the woods, and the slayer of bears and Indians." We saw this singular man for the first time in 1818, and so different was his figure, complexion, and personal appearance from what <u>we</u> had "figured" him to be, that we were struck and wrapt in astonishment. He was rather below the ordinary stature, neat in his person, rather florid for a man of years, a "cheerful expression", and seemed as inoffensive as a child.

[p. 31³]
His voice was mild, and his mind appeared as unruffled as the prairies in the summer, over which he had so often roamed. His eyesight having become too dim to direct the rifle with unerring aim, for a number of years he had forsaken the haunts of the buffaloe, deer, and bear, and domesticated himself with his children, who treated him with affectionate care. We have seen a <u>caracature</u> of Boon as a portrait, and a few years since an engraver produced a plate, and an engraving. It is anything else than Daniel Boon. And why should it be otherwise? The portrait was taken, and the print made, after the grave had concealed him from mortal

[p. 31⁴]
vision. We have noticed the same inaccuracy of expression on the sculptured marble which decorates the

Rotunda of the Capitol at Washington, as the representation of the siege of Boonsborough, Kentucky.

"The article "On the use of tobacco" is deserving the attention of every chewer, smoker, and snuffer in the state. <u>We speak that we do know</u>, when we affirm that the use of tobacco in any or all its modes, is a dirty, disgraceful habit; an outrage upon civilization and Christianity; a habit to which no young man ought ever become addicted; and which every old man ought to quit — <u>if he can</u>! After indulging (with an occasional recess)

[p. 31⁵]

in the smoke of this noxious weed for about nineteen years we came to the conclusion last summer to break off. It cost little more than an unyielding resolution and a few weeks perseverance, to deliver the editor of the Pioneer from the fumes of tobacco smoke and with his present feelings there is little danger of a relapse.

"The article alluded to in the Magazine, is from the pen of the Rev. Dr. Stuart, of the Andover Institution, in the form of a review of a work by Dr. McAlister on the subject."

[p. 32]
<u>Memos.</u>
The four pages following were notes of conversations, noted down at the time, taken during a visit to me in August, 1857, by Rev. Dr. John M. Peck; & the page references refer to Dr. Peck's <u>Life of Boone</u>, in Spark's Biography.

L. C. D.

[p. 33]
<u>Memos of Col. Boone,</u> from conversations with Rev.

<u>John M. Peck</u>, at Madison, Wis. Aug. 12-13th 1857.

P. 174 of this volume, abt. Boones visit to Ky. Got this narrative from Flanders Callaway, & has it recorded in his (Peck's) diary; did not get it in his visit in 1846.

P. 175: Robbed by the Osages, got this incident from Col. D Boone himself, or F. Callaway. This is all he knows of it.

P. 175-6, incident on Green River; got from Dl. Boone, & confirmed by Flanders Callaway.

P. 176-177: hunting on Osage — got from Col. Dl. Boone, but more particularly from F. Callaway; & also

[p. 33¹]

heard it related at Nathan Boone's: At this latter place, learned that they were fond of asking the negro, if Col. B. had died, whether he wd. have ventured to have buried him according to directions? His reply was always evasive — could never be got to say, that he wd. have buried him, nor wd. he say he would have left him unburied.

P. 141-144: the tobacco story — got it from John Welch, a brother of Rev. Rev. Jas. E. Welch, in 1846. John Welch resides near his brother, in Mo., & was present at the wedding, & heard Col. Boone

[p. 33²]

relate the story, at a wedding of a granddaughter of Boone's; & when Welch related it, Mr. Peck was noting it down, other persons present said they were also present at the wedding & heard Col. Boone relate it.

P. 127: Blue Licks — carried off his son, mortally wounded; son gasping, & told his father to leave him & make his escape; & left him almost dead, probably before reaching the river: that the big Indian, was portly, whom he shot in the body, while he, Boone, was carrying off his son, & fell dead. Boone said he

[p. 33³]
always disliked the idea of killing human beings — taking life when we cd. not restore it. Said he had killed the Negro at the Big Siege of Boonesborough; & thus one & two other Indians, but Dr. Peck don't recollect of his telling where he killed these two latter.

[p. 34]
Letter from R. Babcock
Patterson   26th Nov. 1859

My dear Draper: In replying, though hurriedly, to your favor of the 16th inst. I have to say, that I am now employed on the last dozen years of Dr. Peck's life, and have this morning reached the journey of the autumn of 1846 into Missouri to find out if there was anything more which he could learn from Boon's descendants. That effort was a failure. I give you the whole of it in his identical words. Under date of Oct.5th he says "After night, reached Thomas Howell's and tarried. His wife was a daughter of Flanders Callaway, and a stupid old body. Few of Boon's descendants can give me any information about the family. The old woman gave me no Sopper. My horse fared no better, and next morning she charged me 25 cents. I promise never to call here again." This is literally all which he obtained, so far as the Journal showed, by this long journey into that neighborhood for the purpose of completing his information of the Boone family.

The earlier notices from 1818 to 1834 I have been over months ago; but my conviction is strong that they contain in amount nothing but what he has used in his Memoir in Sparks's Biography. I am too much in a hurry just now to go through the reinvestigation of that matter. But some weeks hence, when I have got through the present hurry of Meeting House building and finishing and dedicating and can command a day's time for this purpose I will look over those journals if you particularly desire it, though I am pretty confident the result will be "Nil."

How much I regret your failure of reelection, though a Wisconsin brother by my Side, Rev. Mr Mulhern, says it was all because you were on the Democratic ticket. That he and many other Baptists in the State have been greatly aggrieved by the failure to elect you, that he and others did what they could, by putting your name on the other ticket &c. But such is the frequent result of political complications.

Give my best regards to the Gennetts. Their daughter is doing finely at Pokeepsie. Is Mr Loping still connected with you in the publication of your books? I shall see him next week at Pokeepsie, I have no doubt; and if you would rather have him examine the Journals of Peck he can do so, at any time.

Jones is well, full of legal business, but as much in law with historical and antiquarian research as ever. Have you seen Dr. Spague's vi^th vol of Annals of Am Pulpit, embracing Baptists? It will much please you. Peck did some & Jones & I much more in it.

... in too much hurry

R. Babcock

[p. 35]
Letter from Jas. E. Welch

Wright City, Warren Co. Mo.   May 16 / 61
Dear Bro. D.

Yours of the 26th ult. was duly recd, & in reply, I would say, that my Bro. John now living near me, informs me, that while attending the marriage by Jack Callaway Esq. of the youngest daughter of Flanders Callaway, to Dr. Jones, at the house of her father, which stood on the banks of the Missouri river near Marthaville, in 1818. Old Col. D. Boone her grandfather was present, & related the following adventure, for the amusement of the company.

"When I lived," said he, "on Boone's creek in Ky," (not far from where Roger's mill was afterwards built) "I raised a few hundred plants of tobacco for my own use, to house which, I built a rail pen, high enough for two tier of sticks; cut out about three feet of two or three rails for a door, & wattled in hickory poles, to supply the place of door facings. About one half of my tobacco, ripened before the rest; which I cut & hung upon the lower tier of rails or poles. When I cut the ballance, and took it to the pen, I found it necessary to raise the sticks of very dry tobacco, from the lower to the upper tier, to make room for my newly cut tobacco. While thus engaged & almost done, except three or four more sticks — my head up among the tobacco, so that I could see no where else, except right under me, I was surprized to see four Indians standing.

One of them said to me, "come down, we have catched you two or three times, & you have got away from us; we've got you safe this time". I said to them: well, wait 'till

[p. 35¹]
I hang up these other four sticks, & then I'll come down. I kept my hands above as though I was fixing the upper

sticks while with one foot, I slipt the four sticks of dry tobacco, off from one of the poles & on to the other foot, & while they were standing right under me, I slipt my foot from under, & threw myself upon the four sticks of dry tobacco, and went down with them upon their heads. .

That mashed the tobacco, which so filled their eyes & confused them, that I jumped out at the door & ran, & when about one hundred yards off, I looked back & saw them, still feeling about the pen, trying to find me, when I laughed to myself, & then ran off".

My "Reminiscences" are in Statu quo; such a pressure on the book trade, that I have concluded to wait for a change of times. Dr. Babcock has Peck's memoirs ready for the press, I suppose, but can prevail on no respectable printer to assume the responsibility of publishing it. I spent 10 days at Patterson N. J. two years ago aiding Dr. B. on Peck's life.

We should be glad to see you in these diggings; you will of course call to see us, 6 miles south of Wright City, on the North Mo. R. Road. I preach every Sab.; until lately, had charge of 3 Chs., one 66 miles off at Mexico, another 2 m. off at Troy & two Sab. to our Ch. near home. I have resigned at Mexico one month ago. Mrs. Welch's health is very feeble, mine good. My son & only living child is a mem. of the State Con. & the Legislature & he & I strong Union men.

Lord save our country. Yr &c   Jas. E. Welch

[p. 36]

Information from <u>Isaac Newton Piggott</u>, St. Louis, Mo. (born Nov. 20th, 1793)

<u>Col. John Moredock</u>. In 1803 or 1804, very Early one morning, some guns were heard to crack (I think Mr. Piggott said he heard them, & that they were from the

firing of Moredock's party. Thinks there were twelve of Moredock's party, & as many Indians. There was one Creamer among Moredock's men, a famous gunsmith.

The Indians were on an island (westward of Columbia, in Monroe County, Ills.,) in the Mississippi, close to the Illinois shore [Fine's Island? It wd. seem to me so; see Columbia on Map of Western States — would make a western direction strike the river some little distance above the mouth of Merrimac; & the Ohio & Missi. Navigator, shows Fine's Isld. as the first above the Merrimac, 3½ miles. L. C. D.] A small slough was necessary to cross to reach the island: The Indians were supposed to be a set of thieving fellows, a mixed gang, stole & did mischief. An Indian snapped his gun at Creamer, & it missed fire; & it used to be said, that it was not a gun of Creamer's make, for his locks never missed fire.

It was astonishing that no white was killed or wounded. Indians made some resistance; one Indian jumped into the river, when two of the whites jumped into a canoe, pursued & killed him. The other Indians were shot & killed on the spot. No notice was ever taken of Moredock & his party by civil authorities; nor did the Indians show any resentment.

Moredock's mother killed. She was killed, & her body cut open by the Indians: The Indians had long before killed Moredock's father; & about the time his mother was killed, they also killed his step-father, John Huff.

At the treaty of Portage Des Sioux, in 1815, Moredock

[p. 37]
said the Americans might make peace if they pleased, but he never would as long as he lived. Gov. Clark had deliv-

ered each head chief a medal, and an American flag. There was present a tribe who had been warlike & refractory, now very humble, begging for peace and presents. Then a salute was fired with three cannon, so suddenly that the chief of these refractory Indians, partly fell with his flag presented to him, when Murdock exclaimed: "See the villainous, cowardly, guilty rascal; he shows guilt, & ought to be killed on the spot." The Commissioners quieted Moredock. These refractory Indians were very likely the Sauks. Mr. Piggott was present.

New Design.. I have a new design to go out and settle at such a place, said James Lemon Sr., & hence the place was called New Design.

See Amn. State Papers, 1st. Vol., abt. 15th page, on Public Lands: the petition of James Piggott & others to Gov. St. Clair for land.

Of Sig-ge-nauk, or Later-nean, the Indian Chief, no knowledge; he must have died early.

Piggott's Fort was established in 1783; was the first American settlement, hiving out from Kaskaskia; & the French people would describe the settlement as "the bottom where the Americans were" — & finally, for short, the American Bottom.

Tom Brady. Don't know his origin. He was living in 1799; can't say how much later. It was always a general belief among the aged people, that Brady did go on an Expedition to St. Joseph. Gov. Reynold's account is substantially correct, derived from Nichs. Boismenue, a reliable man, who has been Several years dead.

Whitesides Attack on Indians, Feb. 1793 [See Peck's edn. Western Annals, p. 703]. The Whitesides always wished to attack everything in the shape of Indians; others thought they ought to refrain, & cultivate peaceful

[p. 38]

relations with the Indians. They attacked <u>Pecau</u> & party; Pecau perhaps wounded, & several Indians killed, under the bluff, between Cahokia, & now Belleville. Some thought this attack a wanton act. Can't say what became of Pecau, who was highly regarded.

<u>Attack on St. Louis, 1780.</u> Always understood from the old people, Clark had inculcated the idea that his troops in Illinois were only the advance guard — his main army at the Falls of Ohio. The old French, & Spanish also, believed it; and so related it to the Indians, and they dreaded Clark. Some Americans at Cahokia marched out, & the Indians believing if Clark got after them they would all be killed, hence fled. Can give no facts about the number killed at St. Louis. Mr. Piggott discredits the story of Leyba being bribed. Has no knowledge of Miss Leyba. The old French & Spanish people were very superstitious, hence doubtless the bribery story finding credence with some of them. No doubt some information was given the Indians by some one, that Clark's host would be upon them, & none would survive his terrible onslaught.

<u>Fort Jefferson Attacks, 1781.</u> Gov. Reynolds, in his <u>Life & Times</u> has given quite a narrative of Ft. Jefferson; he got but a part of his matter from informant, (Mr. Piggott), but mostly from the Lemons, who were in Piggott's Fort, & got their knowledge from the Fort Jefferson men who lived in the fort, & from Mrs. Nancy Phelps, of Belleville, who as a child was there, daughter of Jacob Judy.

Capt. Jas. Piggott, Judy & Henry Mace, Wm. Murray, Sib. Cummins, George Lunceford, & _____ Strode, were among the Fort Jefferson defenders, & perhaps James More & family.

What Mann Butler relates in his <u>Hist. of Kentucky</u>, from Mr. Donne, a youth, is quite erroneous, so Butler since said to informant.

Col. G. R. Clark persuaded Jas. Piggott, (who had

[p. 39]

been with Gen. St. Clair in 1777 — a Captain then, & left the Service to go & protect the frontiers, & his exposed family — & so went to West Pa., & then down to Falls of Ohio) to go with a colony to Fort Jefferson; Piggott had visited Kentucky in 1778, and joined Clark & went with him, same as Capt. Wm. Linn, as an independent volunteer, & was with him in his conquest of Illinois — taking of Kaskaskia &c.

Don't know the number of persons who settled at Fort Jefferson, nor the number of the garrison. Adam Strode had a desperate personal conflict with an Indian outside the fort, the Indian trying to cut Strode's throat, & did actually succeed in wounding him (informant saw the scar); but the Indian in some way got his knife broken, or dropped it, and Strode stabbed & killed him. Strode died at an early day, in Illinois, perhaps not long after the war of 1812-'15.

During the siege of Fort Jefferson, it was very sickly, & the people were in much want of food.

When the Indians first came there, Cummins said a council was called. Colbert, the white leader of the Chickasaws, came with a flag of truce, and halted at a respectful distance; several officers went out with Capt. Piggott to meet Colbert & several chiefs with him; wouldn't let them come into the fort, to discover their weakness. Colbert demanded the surrender of the fort without conditions, promising, however, to use his influence with the Indians, and he thought they would not injure any of the prisoners — urging their surrender as the only hope for their safety, as he knew resistance would be utterly useless, as he had, he said, upwards of 1200 of the best Indian warriors, whom he was restraining from their eagerness

[p. 40]
to commence the attack. He added, that the Indians had taken a prisoner, and from him had learned their numbers and situation; he even informed us, said Colbert, where your cannon are posted, and that you have not amunition enough to fire them twice [which was true], & then described the situation of the fort & its arrangements accurately. He cautioned them that they need not flatter themselves that they would ever get the amunition and supplies they had sent for, for a large force had been sent to intercept the expected convoy, and would certainly effect it.

It was true, as Piggott & his companions said, that Clark's men were invincible; but they could not hope successfully to resist without amunition or food?

At this juncture, two of Piggott's men evinced palor and fear, and seemed to think that a surrender might, under the circumstances, be the wisest course. Piggott brushed back his gray hair with his fingers, and said substantially:

Captain Colbert, I wish you to inform your Indians that Clark's men have never yet been defeated. It is not necessary to make any answer to what you say your prisoner has reported to you, as he would naturally enough try to conciliate your favorable consideration by saying whatever might seem desirable to you. You say we have settled here on your territory without your consent. Now, if you will peaceably withdraw, we will agree to leave the country; but if you attack us, you will find that we will fight it out, and never give up. We have a fort in which to defend ourselves, and we can kill ten of you to your one of us. You ask us to surrender. That we will never do, for we cannot

[p. 41]

rely on Indian pledges of good treatment, for the Indians killed a number of our people after they surrendered at Ruddell and Martin's Stations, last year, in Kentucky.

Then Colbert went to consult with the Indians, deploring the obstinacy and recklessness of the whites, in bringing swift destruction on their heads. Just as he turned away, two of the Americans who could split an apple with their rifles at a hundred yards, fired from their concealment outside the fort, unknown to any of the officers, one aiming at Colbert's medal on his breast, & failed; the other gave him a flesh wound in the arm. These men excused themselves from the treacherous act by asserting that Colbert was looking at the fort to gain information by observation. Colbert now appealed to Piggott and the officers to protect him under the sacredness of the flag. So Piggott & the men with him bound up his wound, condemning & regretting the occurrence, & promising to look into the matter, saying to Colbert, "You see how impatient Clark's soldiers are to commence the fight." Colbert & party were then escorted and protected to a safe distance beyond the reach of danger.

The Indians then held, at a proper distance, but within view of the fort, a council, which was prolonged till night. Just after the interview, & before night, the expected relief arrived safely, without the Indians discovering it; their intercepting party had probably struck the Ohio too high up, after the relief had passed. This was the real means of success. After dark the Indians attacked the fort. The American fired their cannon repeatedly, to prove to their enemies that they had plenty of amunition.

Reynold's account is right, except informant has no recollection about a man running out

[p. 42]
of the fort & killing the Indian who was trying to set the fort on fire; yet it may have been so. It was a desperate fight. The Indians retired, expecting the whites would abandon the place.

Don't know what the Indians did with their prisoner.

Layton White was probably at Fort Jefferson; dont know when he died.

Mrs. Nancy Phelps, from whom Gov. Reynolds chiefly got his details of the attack on Fort Jefferson, resided in or near Belleville; was a daughter of Jacob Judy, a sister of Col. Saml. Judy. She was old enough to observe & relate the incidents as she witnessed them & was doubtless reliable. Her father, Jacob Judy, married Betsey Wheat for his second wife, at Piggott's Station, in the American Bottom. She was rough, fearless woman, and had somewhere distinguished herself in defence of some fort [at Wheeling, in Sept. 1782. — L. C. D.] She had previous to this marriage a natural son, George Green, but had no children by Judy. She died in St. Louis county, Mo., about 1820.

There was a man named Musick at Fort Jefferson; thinks his first name was William; he was a very rough man; settled & died in Missouri.

In 1838, Isc. N. Piggott petitioned Congress for pay for military services of Capt. James Piggott — that in addition to service as Captain in 1776 and 1777, "he was in two battles with the Indians at the Iron Banks". Two depositions taken before the Mayor of St. Louis, of <u>James McMeans</u> and <u>Jacob Swaney</u> (on Merrimack, Mo., testifying that they were acquainted with Captn. Piggott in 1780-'81 or '82, and were members of his company of volunteers, and that Capt. Piggott was in actual service against the Indians on the Western frontiers, under Genl. George Rogers Clark.

[p. 43]

The committee reported adversely June 9, 1837.

Mr. Piggott says he knows nothing about the "two battles" referred to at the Iron Banks, or Fort Jefferson, but feels confident they must have occurred at the same siege.

When Capt. Piggott left Fort Jefferson, with several families in company, they went to Kaskaskia, & lived there awhile; then went & lived awhile at Cahokia, then went and settled Piggott's Fort at Great Run.

Capt. Piggott was commissioned Captain April 6, 1776, of second battalion of Military Associators of Westmoreland County, Pa., by the Pennsylvania Assembly, signed John Morton, Speaker.

Incident. <u>Jacob Grotz</u>, & one Watt left Piggott's Fort, afraid of Indians in the Illinois country, & made arrangements to move to St. Louis as a greater place of safety: Had been to St. Louis, & returned to Piggott's, & both started on horseback, & had gone three or four miles towards Cahokia, when they were waylaid by Indians, & shot at as they were riding unconcernedly along the pathway. Watt was mortally wounded, but his horse carried him off to Cahokia, where he died. Grotz was not wounded, but thrown from his horse, holding on to the bridle. He was a very powerful man; both Indians dropped their guns, & attempted to catch the horse.

Grotz' foot was fastened in the stirrup, & he hung to the bridle, which made the horse circle around. Indians rushed up & stabbed him, & he knocked them down repeatedly, & made a desperate defence in his hampered condition, but they finally killed him.

Col. David Musick waived his rank as Colonel, & went up with a volunteer company, informant one, in perhaps 1814, on a scout up the Mississippi, all in boats; went only part way up the river.

Col. Dickson. It was understood that as soon as the British took New Orleans, then Dickson was to go & take St. Louis, & sweep the whole country So the traders & half breeds reported. No foundation for the report against Maj. Ths. Forsyth as favoring Dickson in his contemplated movement.

Capt. John Miller commanded a company, & informant was orderly sargeant in it, to guard the Commrs. at treaty of Portage Des Sioux in 1815; from St. Louis County.

Creve Coeur — could have been no massacre there in 1780. May 29-31 & June 1st 60

[p. 44]

Request of James Piggott to resign from military service

(Copy.)

To His Excellency George Washington, commander in chief of the Armies of the United States of America:

The petition of James Piggott Humbly Sheweth that your petitioner was appointed a Captain in the Eighth Penna. Regt., in which station he would still continue with pleasure to act; but finding my health much impaired, and being informed of hostilities, ravages & murders being committed on the inhabitants near the river

Ohio; that your petitioner's family & effects are in the most exposed parts of that country, your petitioner therefore begs leave

[p. 45]
to resign his commission in order that he may give some relief to his family that otherwise are destitute of any; & your petitioner as in duty bound will ever pray, &c.

James Piggott.

[Appended to above:]
I do hereby certify that Captn. James Piggott is not indebted to the regiment according to my best knowledge.

Matthew Jack, Capt.

Sir:
    I do hereby certify that I believe the facts stated in the above petition, as well as in Captn. Jack's certificate, to be true.

Danl. Brodhead, Col. 8th Penn. Regt.

His Excellency Genl. Washington.

[p. 46]
    Camp 22d Oct. 1777.
    For the within reasons His Excellency Genl. Washington has accepted of Capt. Piggott's resignation, but he is first to deliver his commission as Captain in the 8th. Pa. Regt. to Col. Brodhead.

Rich. Humpton, Col.
Comandng. 2d, B.G.
Lincoln's division.

Pennsylvania S.S.
    To all whom it doth or may concern:

Thomas Scott, Esquire, Member of the Supreme Executive Council of the Said State, sends greeting:

Know ye that the bearer hereof, Captain James Piggott, is a true friend of the United State of America, in whose cause he hath acquitted himself

[p. 47]
well as an officer, and also hath been a regular subject of this State, whereof he hath produced me, besides my own knowledge, sufficient testimony; & having occasion to move with his family & effects to Kentucky in the State of Virginia. These are therefore to recommend him to passage & safe conduct on his way thither, &c.

Given under my hand & seal at Westmoreland County, the tenth day of April, anno domini, 1779.

Tho. Scott.

Note by the copyist, whose copy I transcribe: "The 1779 in the above I think to be correct; not certain."

[p. 48]
Permit for James Piggott and others to pass to Falls of Ohio

Youghigania County, Va.

Pass Capt. James Piggott & Jesse Rude, Daniel Meredith, Reuben Watt with their families, & James Williams, single man, hath applied to us to pass from hence to the Falls of Ohio, or the new settlements near that place, they having shewn to us sufficient certificates of their good behavior in other places of their abode, & a copy of their oath of allegiance & fidelity agreeable to act of the Genl. Assembly of the State, & nothing appearing to us why they may not be permitted to pass.

Edward Ward.
Thos. Smallman.

[p. 49]

These are therefore to require all or any of the leige officers, civil or military of our State, where the said James Piggott, Jesse Rude, Daniel Meredith, Reuben Watts, & James Williams, May have or require to go, to suffer them to pass or repass on their lawful occasion; they demeaning & behaving themselves, agreeable to the laws & customs of the place of the trust confided in them.

Given under our hands at Pittsburgh in the State &c, this 17th day of May, in the year of our Lord, 1779.

Provided they have neither deserters nor publick property on board their craft.

To all concerned.

> Danl. Brodhead
> Col. Commanding
> Western Department.

[p. 50]

Killed & Wounded. St. Clair's Defeat

Nov. 4, 1791.

List of Killed:

Maj. Ferguson	}	
Capt. Bradford	}	Artillery.
Lieut. Spear	}	
Maj. Heart	}	
Capt. Philson	}	
" Newman	}	
" Kirkwood	}	
Lieut. Warren	}	
" Balch	} 2d Rifle	
Ensign Cobb	} Regt. Levies	
Capt. Swearingen	}	
" Stemton	}	

"   Pine or Price   }
Lieut. Boyd   }
Ensigns Chase, Reeves   }
Wilson, Rooks, Turner   }
Actr/Buvers
     Grayson

Killed & Wounded, St. Clair's Defeat.

Capt. Cribbs	}	
" Pratt	}	
" Smith	}	
" Purdy	}	2d
Lieuts.: Linaus	}	Regt.
" Kelso	}	Levies.
Ensigns M Michaes	}	
" Bealey	}	
" Purdy	}	
Adjt. Anderson	}	

Lieut. Col. Oldham	}	
Capt. Leman	}	Kentucky
Lieut. Briggs	}	Militia.
Ens. Montgomery	}	

List of Wounded:
Capt. Ford
     Imman
Lieut. De Butto
Cornet Bines
Capt. Doyle, 1st Regt.
Lieut. Col. Dark
Capt. Dark

Wounded, continued:

Lieut. Lisle
   "   Thompson
       Morgan
       Reed
       Rhea
       Commings.
       Larison
Ens. Morehead
       Prue
Adjt. Rawford
   "   Whistle
Capt. Thomas
Lt. Col. Gibson
Capt. Madison
Maj. Butler
Lieut. Downs
Capt. Slough
— Hagner
Ensign Waller
Dr. Garns
Maj. Genl. Butler Killed.
Adjt. Gen. Sergeant wounded
Viscount, aid de camp to

Genl. St.. Clair, wounded.

N.B. Of the 1st Regt. there was only a small detachment in the action, the regt. being on command. The number killed in the whole is said to be 840. Majr Hamtramck is returned to the post with 35 men.

Nothing further has transpired.

Govr. St. Clair went immediately to Congress.

From yr. humble servt.

        B. Tardiveau:

You will oblige me to forward the enclosed.

To Capt. James Piggott

    Great Run."

    [Illinois]

[p. 54]

Rules & Regulations with regard to the Fort at the Great Run

    — in reference to the 2d constitution thereof by the people.

    No cause of action for the resons following: Piggott missing the door had a right to inquire after it, nor could he do his duty as a justice of the peace, or the militia officer commanding in that fort, without inquiring and bringing the offender to trial, for the following reasons:

    That Fort was Established under certain rules and conditions by the mutual consent and approbation of each inhabitant, certified under their hands the 2d of March, 1789, which proves that no person had a right to diminish

[p. 55]

any part of the Fort or other improvements, but leave them thus forever. That Huff did unhinge & carry away from a corner house [a door], is proved by his own confession; that he did it in a clandestine manner is evident also, as there were near thirty people living in the fort, & none of them saw Huff take the door. That Huff was a disorderly person, & his house suspected for secreting stolen property, can be proved by Sheriff Biggs & others while he lived in the fort, & that they have been troublesome neighbors where they now live is their general character.

That the house and door in dispute was fixed to the Fort after the formation of the Constitution for that Fort, at which time Piggott had no power to dispose of, plan,

[p. 56]
or order the planning or removing of any house or building in or about the Fort whatever.

That Piggott was not the cause of rendering void the constitution of the Great Run Fort, but always showed a willingness to support the rules & live orderly under them, is evident.

The manner how the first Constitution became void is certified in the conditions of residence for the year following, & that by more than 20 subscribers.

That Piggott had a desire to prevent confusion, & keep in their purity the privileges and benefits of the people is evidently proved by the verdict of the trustees the 26th of September, 1790, which verdict hath been a rule

[p. 57]
to Piggott ever since, & so to continue."

Mr. I. N. Piggott remarks the above was John Huff, the Step father of Col. Moredock. Sd. Huff was a bad character; & when killed by the Indians, Moredock said he was sorry the Indians killed him; nevertheless they saved him the trouble of killing him, yet he wd. kill an Indian in retalation

It was at Great Run Fort the cannon was fired that scared the Indians who captured Wm. Biggs. The cannon there were brought up from Ft. Jefferson.

There was some difficulties between French in Ills. & Amns., & hence this settlement at Great Run.

When Gov. St. Clair came, he consulted his old Pa. friend Piggott & took his advice in making the apptmts.

for St. Clair County.

[p. 58]
Notes on Piggott's Fort
From Mrs. <u>Asenath Patterson</u>, residing near Florissant, St. Louis Co, Mo., daughter of Capt. James Piggott, & Hannah Ballou James, born in Piggott's Fort or Block House, on the American Bottom, & near the present village of Columbia, 9 miles from Cahokia, in Monroe Co., Ills., Jan. 17, 1791.

<u>Col. John Moredock's Fight</u> took place near Piggott's Fort when informant was about twelve years old. She heard the screams, as she distinctly remembers. Moredock headed a crowd. Those beside him were shy about acknowledging their participation in the affair. Nothing was ever done with Moredock for it.

Capt. <u>Piggott</u> served under Washington, but no particulars recollected; & nothing remembered about events in the Red Stone country.

<u>Piggott's Fort</u> had eighteen families, besides young men, & all had their corn ground on a hand mill. All their horses were stolen by the Indians, & cattle also; & had to make corn with the hoe.

Mrs. Patterson says her mother was the widow of Bennet Ballou, who was killed by the Indians when travelling; & thinks her father, Capt. Piggott married her in Illinois; that informant was the seventh child, and all the children were born in Illinois. Her mother died in St. Louis in June, about 1833.

Capt. Piggott was but little short of six feet, with black hair, blue eyes, fair skin. Died opposite St. Louis, at Piggott's Ferry, and was [p. 58[1]]

buried at Cahokia.

Jacob Grots lived in Piggott's Fort, had a family there, & was killed when returning from St. Louis.

May 22d & 23d. 1868.

For further notice of Capt. Piggott, see Gov. Reynolds' Life & Times.

See Hist. Westmoreland Co. Pa. pp. 87, 88, 456.

An article in Notes & Queries, Oct. 14, 1882, p. 309, shows a prominent Piggott family in Queen's County, Ireland, in the middle of the eighteenth century.

[p. 59]

Report of Revolutionary Claims Committee

Capt. James Piggott. June 9, 1838, the comtee. on Revolutionary claims, to whm. was referred the petition of Isaac N. Piggott, asking pay for military services of Captain James Piggott, deceased, report:

"It appears, from the Evidence submitted to the committee, that on the 6th day of April, 1776, James Piggott was appointed a Captain of a company of foot, and commissioned by the General Assembly of the then Province of Pennsylvania, in the second battalion of the military associators in the county of Westmoreland, for the protection of the then province against all hostile enterprises, and for the defence of American liberty; that, on the 22d day of October, 1777, Captain Piggott resigned his commission, and the same day was duly accepted by General Washington, as appears by document marked with the letter C.

"It is alleged in the petition, that subsequent to the resignation of Captai iggott (but at what time is not stated) he raised a company of volunteers, and entered the regiment commanded by Colonel George Rogers Clark;

that this regiment proceeded down the Ohio river, and near a place then known as the <u>Iron Banks</u>, on the Mississippi river, <u>Captain Piggott</u>, with

[p. 60]

the said regiment, was engaged in two battles with the Indians; that Captain Piggott from thence ascended that river to several points; that at Grand River his company erected a small place of defence, and known as "Piggott's Block House", now in St. Clair County, State of Illinois. It is further alleged in the petition that Captain Piggott was actively engaged in the service of his country in subduing the Savages on the Western frontier, and defending it against their hostile invasions, and continued in Such Service until the cessation of hostilities on the part of the Indians. It does not appear at what time this service terminated.

"Two depositions taken before the Mayor of St. Louis, Missouri, have been Submitted to the committee. The names of the affiants are <u>James McMeans</u> and <u>Jacob Swancy</u>; both of these persons swear that they were acquainted with Captain Piggott in the years 1780, '81, and '82, and both swear they were Members of Captain Piggott's company of volunteers, and that Captain Piggott was in actual service against the Indians on the Western frontier, and that his company was a part of the regiment of Gen. George Rogers Clark.

"The committee report against the prayer of the petitioner". <u>Revolutionary Claims</u>, 8vo., p. 485, 486.

[p. 61]
Letters from Isaac Newton Piggott
St. Louis Nov. 27

Lyman C. Draper Esqr.
Madison Wis.
Dear Sir:

Your letter of inquiry &c of 14th October came
to hand. I will give the desired information as soon as I
have the time to do so; until then accept this brief &c.

I, am the only surviving son of Capt. James Piggott
who defended Fort Jefferson against an attack of the Indians in 1781. The account as given by Gov. Reynolds of
Illinois is substantially correct as far as it goes, (see history of Reynolds' life and times, Pages 53 to 60). But I
have some old documents and writings, some of which
can be read and others only in part, yet they will aid in
supporting a correct Traditional historical account of
those great events which transpired in what was then
called the Territory N.W. of the River Ohio. I will remark that Mr. Butler who wrote the History of Kentucky,
had discovered the strange Elipsis & apparent confli ting
statements of Historians with regard to the History   ie
West; and had made the same request of me which you
now make and I had commenced preparing a Synopsis of
the facts for him When his death put an end to the work.
It has been perceived that although Historians could get
the facts tolerably correct in the old states with regard to
them, yet they could not get the facts with regard to what
transpired in this, their Savage Wilderness; From 1781 to
1790 there is almost no reliable history of Illinois; nothing but scraps of history appears, for instance, Although
Gov. Henry (of Va.) instructions to Col. G. R. Clark, as
well as other Histories show the facts that not only the
conquest of Illinois was contemplated by the confidential
parties, but it was then in 1778 a part of the great scheme
of Gov. Henry and his confidential advisers as well as
Genl. Clark to establish a post on the Mississippi River

below the mouth of the Ohio, which it is said Clark

[p. 61¹]
effected in 1780, notwithstanding the strong dissatisfac-
tion of the inhabitants of Kentucky &c. and that said Fort
was successfully defended against the combined attack of
the Choctaw & Chicasaw Indians.

Now Sir: it is well known that the U.S. Government
never sent any Troops there, and that Col. Clarks men
were only enlisted for 3 months which had expired in
1778. Yet no Historian except Gov. Reynolds has attempted to inform us who those men were, from where
they came, and what became of them. Who has written
their epitaph? and where is it to be found. I ask again
what Historian has given any natural account of how this
great Territory was retained for the U.S. from 1781 to
1790. An account of such strange omissions the unwary
reader might suppose the Brittish Lion had become a
Lamb, and his allies the Tigerlike Savage had lost his
thirst for human Blood. But the facts were the opposite
and every year was full of Tragical events.

If you want I will write out a synopsis of the material
facts from the time Clark came on here to 1799. You will
please inform me your wish in this matter. The Jarrot of
whom you speak in your letter still resides here, and I
will call on her and make inquiry as requested.

Yours Very Respectfully
Isaac Newton Piggott

[p. 62]
St. Louis Jan. 28th. 1865
Lyman C. Draper Esqr.
Dear Sir,
please pardon my omition of Duty. Being old, feble,

& surrounded with exitenging Seens of the present war, I neglected to finish the Synopticle Sketch, which I had began, of the former wars, in which the 1st. American settlements of the N.W. were envolved. But you will see by the enclosed slips from the Bellville Advocate, that I have not forgotten the subject, but I find it requires much more labour, & research than at first siposed, to supply historicle Ellipses, & straten their conflicting statements & you will see from my spelling & scrol that where I was braught up there was no oppertunity to git an education, hence I srank from the task. Yet on your patience has not entirely failed. I will again resume, with however the understanding, that I be allowe to abbreviate ... & by reference to ohers already in history enable you to supply even my Ellipses.

[p. 62¹]
You see that I comenced this letter on 28th Jan. but I have been to Ill to go on with the writing untill now Feb. 13th. 1865 So, I will now send you this in advance hopeing you will make due allowance for my delay. I will soon send you the Copies of some old documents & a condensed sketch of the lief of my father Capt. James Piggott.

I am sir with great Respect
Your most obdient Servt.
I. N. Piggott

[p. 63]
The Weekly Advocate.
G. F. Kimball, Editor.
Friday, April 17, 1863.
Belleville, Illinois.
Early History of St. Clair County.
Saint Louis, April 10, 1863.
Hon. John Reynolds, Ex-Gov. Of Illinois:

Although you, like myself, stand on the eve of life, yet I see in the Belleville *Democrat* of the 21st of March last, that you are taking a retrospective view of early life in Illinois, in which you give a "picture" of St. Clair county in A.D. 1800. You promise at some future time to brush up your "picture" in detail, in which I hope you will make some corrections, so that those who were first may not appear last. For, although you have written more fully than former historians with regard to the acquisition and defense of Illinois up to the year 1800, yet in some instances you have been too much led by them — who at the time they wrote had no means of fully understanding many things that transpired in the savage wilderness from A.D. 1777 to 1800, hence many facts they could not mention, and others are so blended that they are not well understood, and blame is sometimes attached where praise should have been awarded, &c.

I think with you, sir, that those historical ellipses should now be supplied, so as to furnish a full and unblended history of matters and things, so that those who at their own expense bore the burden, and by their labor, suffering and blood, retained and defended this country from the year 1778 to 1800. [Marginal handwritten note: should be correctly reported.] Nor is it any reflection on former historians, who did all they could to obtain and give correct information; and, so far as the old States are concerned, have done so, and on their works we expect to draw, but as we have said it was then impossible for them to obtain full and correct information of the many tragical scenes that transpired on the Western frontier.

Only reflect on the surroundings of the country when there was no printing, nor post offices, mail carriers, roads, bridges, nor ferries, and scarce enough of writing paper could be obtained on which to write official dispatches. Of course much of the former history had to be gathered from the statements of many who, like Job's messenger, said to him, "They have slain thy servants, &c., and I only am escaped alone to tell thee." All true, but the half has not been told. Now, sir, let us seek for other documents of that date, together with the traditional accounts which were uniformly given by *all* those who took part therein, and as they taught the facts to their children who were born and brought up in and around these forts of the West. And here allow me to enter my protest against the popular error of historians, who palliate the bloody and treacherous ourrages of the Chickasaw and Choctaw Indians on the inhabitants of Fort Jefferson in 1781, alleging that "said Fort was built against their protest, which *provoked* thereon," &c., which I consider a slander against all concerned, whereas it may be considered but a counterpart of that committed last year (1862) by the Indians on the white settlers of Upper Minnesota.

[Marginal handwritten insertion: It is a proverb, that] "A living dog is better than a dead lion," therefore the friends of Colbert, the wealthy Scotchman and Indian Chief, who led the Indians in the charge on Fort Jefferson, got it reported as it is now found in some of our histories.

Why, sir, at that time no formal treaty or purchase could possibly have been accomplished. But a great number of the chiefs had been consulted and fully acquiesced therein, professed friendship, and received gifts, as I have been informed from my youth up by those who took part therein; in fact, sir, the territory on which St. Louis stands, and that on which several other towns had been located, and the surrounding country, were claimed by the Illinois Indians, but they had acquiesced in the intrusion of the whites and had never molested them." (See Western Annals, p. 243.)

Now, sir, as this is intended for general publication, with a view of obtaining all authentic information in regard thereto, I propose the following questions, viz:

1. Did not the original instructions given to Col. G. R. Clark contemplate the building of Fort Jefferson near the mouth of the Ohio river? And for what purpose was it wanted there?

2. As the inhabitants of Kentucky were opposed thereto, deeming it too great a dispersion of their little force, and as the Government never had any regularly organized [marginal handwritten insertion: troops] there, we inquire by whose hands was Fort Jefferson built? who devised the plan thereof? when was it commenced and finished? and who defended it during the awful week in July, 1781, when it was assaulted and besieged by the combined warriors of the Chickasaw and Choctaw Indians, led by Colbert the Scotch savage chief? What became of those veterans, and what has ever been done for them? If correct answers can be obtained to these questions, it will open the door for further information.

I will here suggest the resignation of Capt. James Piggott, who participated throughout the contest, first in the forced marches and hard-fought battles in which our army had been engaged, until Gen. Burgoyne had surrendered the British army at Saratoga prisoners of war to our army, the news of which spread great joy throughout the country. But as the storms of war receded from the East, the more awful it lowered around the Western frontier — but how was best to defend the same was a matter on which the friends of our country differed much. One party wrote to General Washington to send "Col. Crawford, who was an old pioneer, to take active command in the West." But, as had been anticipated by those who held with Col. Clark, all this ended in nothing effectual, nor did it prevent the massacre at Fort Henry and Wheeling; but when the news reached Headquarters, the plan was soon devised by which the resignation of Captain Piggott was effected so that he could also go to their aid, which could not be allowed while he retained office in the regular army, and because it is a document of that date it is herein inserted; viz:

To his Excellency George Washington, Esq., Commander-in-Chief of the Army of the United States of America:

[p. 64]

The petition of James Pigott humbly showeth, that your petitioner was appointed Captain in the Eighth Pennsylvania Regiment, in which station, he would still continue with pleasure to act, but finding my health impaired, and being informed of hostilities, ravages, and murders being committed on the inhabitants near the Ohio river; that your petitioner's family and effects are in the most exposed parts of that country, your petitioner begs leave, therefore, to resign his commission, in order that he may give some relief to his family, that otherwise are destitute of any; and your petitioner as in duty bound will ever pray, &c. JAMES PIGGOTT.

I do hereby certify that Capt. James Piggott is not indebted to the regiment according to my best knowledge.

MATTHEW JACK, Capt.

I do hereby certify that I believe the facts stated in the above petition, as well as in Captain Jack's certificate, to be true.

D. BROADHEAD,
Colonel 8th Penn. Regiment.

His Excellency General Washington.
Camp, Oct. 22, 1777.

For the within reasons his Excellency, General Washington, has accepted of Capt. Piggott's resignation. But he is first to deliver his commission as Captain in the 8th Pennsylvania Regiment to Col. Broadhead.

WILLIAM WASHINGTON.
Col. Commd'g 2d B. G., Lincoln Div.

We perceive the resignation of Capt. Piggott was accepted by

Gen. Washington for the reasons therein set forth; and it is due to the memory of those great officers whose names are connected therewith to say, that they well understood the object of Captain Piggott was not to retire from the service of his country, but to change his location therein. They know that he always made the time of his country's extremity the opportunity to volunteer his services, where they were most needed, without regard to office, or ease for himself. He might have retired with our army into winter quarters at Valley Forge. But he chose to transfer himself to the most exposed part of the Western frontier, where he passed the winter of 1777-8. Meanwhile Col. G. R. Clark went and submitted his great plan for the conquest of the Northwest to Gov. Henry of Virginia, which finally resulted in the acquisition of all the territory of the United States north west of the Ohio river.

To be continued, and at some future time I will try to brush up the picture of Fort Jefferson and the defense of this country from 1781 to 1800.

ISAAC NEWTON PIGGOTT.

[p. 65]

The Belleville Weekly Advocate.
G. F. Kimball, Editor.
Official Paper of the City.
Friday, July 3, 1863.
The Early History of St. Clair.
St. Louis, June 6, 1863.
Hon. John Reynolds, Ex-Governor of Illinois:

Dear Sir: In consequence of the wonderful changes in the natural scenery in the vicinity of St. Louis, Mo., also in the rivers Mississippi and L'Abbe, *alias* Cahokia creek, in St. Clair county, Ill., it is necessary to enable persons who have not been thirty years or over in this part of the country, to comprehend the facts about which we are writing, that we should give some description of its former appearance.

I will, therefore, preface the account which I am about to give with that derived from the late August Chouteau, Sen. (See *Western Annals*, p. 122, from 1764 to 1800):

"At that time a skirt of tall timber lined the bank of the river free from undergrowth which extended back to a line about the range of Eighth street; in the rear was an extensive prairie; the first cabins were erected near the river and Market street; no "Bloody Island," or "Duncan's Island" then existed. Directly opposite the old market square the river was narrow and deep, and until about the commencement of the present century persons could be distinctly heard from the opposite shore. Opposite Duncan's Island and South St. Louis was an island covered with heavy timber and separated from the Illinois shore by a slough. Many persons are now living (1850) who recollect the only ferry from Illinois to St. Louis was from Cahokia, below the island, and landed on the Missouri shore near the site of the United States Arsenal."

It must be noted that previous to A. D. 1800 the said island was joined to the main land at the head thereof, by reason of the filling up of said slough, which had formerly flowed from the Mississippi into the former channel of said creek, between the Cahokia commons on the south and the place where the Belleville railroad forms a junction with the Terre Haute, Alton and St. Louis railroad on the north.

Said creek did not then run into the Mississippi where it now does, but, after receiving said slough, it continued its course down past the village of Cahokia and entered said river at the then (1795) only ferry in this country as above stated.

By reference to the seventy-second page of Mann Butler's *History of Kentucky*, it will be seen that said creek was said to be about knee-deep in front of Col. Clark's camp at Cahokia, when he held his treaty with the Indians in Sept. 1778, but neither slough, creek nor island can now be properly recognized at that place.

But I must resume the former description of the land opposite the city of St. Louis, which at that time laid between said creek and the river, and above (that is) north of the junction of the aforesaid railroads; all the space above that point including the present channel of said creek at the lower railroad bridge, and where those ponds of water now are, both above and below the macadamized dyke, was then high bottom land covered with majestic forest timber, which extended a great way up the river and to the bank thereof, which was then not far from the depots of the several railroads now standing at East St. Louis.

Capt. James Piggott had previously built his cabin at this point, which was then the common camping ground of the Illinois Indians who traded at St. Louis, yet he did not remove his family from his fort at the Great Run, until after Gen. Wagner's treaty with the Indians in 1795.

We must bear in mind that, although Col. Clark in 1778 took all the territory north-west of the river Ohio from the British lion, yet his allies the Indians, like tigers thirsting for blood, still claimed and occupied, and like lords of the forest roamed this vast region of wild country.

And in 1795, when said Piggott first established what is now the Wiggins' ferry, he had at his own expense cut out the first road through what was then a dense forest, and to erect the first bridge across said creek; both of which were essential to his ferry, and then required vastly more time, labor, and expense than they now would; therefore it became necessary that he should have the *exclusive right of ferriage to St. Louis,* or to collect toll at his bridge from all those who had been set over the river by other persons. To settle this question he petitioned Zeno Trudeau, the lieutenant-general of the Spanish province of Upper Louisiana and commandant at St. Louis, who, in consideration of the facts therein stated, did grant to said James Piggott the *exclusive* right of ferriage at St. Louis, and as it is an ancient document I will here insert said petition, which was in the words and figures following, viz:

St. Clair county, territory of the United States, north west of the river Ohio.

To Mr. Zeno Trudeau, commander at St. Louis:

Sir: Though unacquainted, through a certain confidence of your love of justice and equity, I venture to lay before you the following petition, which from reasons following I am confident you will find just to allow.

The petition is, that your honor will grant me the whole benefit of this ferry to and from the town of St. Louis. I do not desire to infringe upon the privilege of the ferry below the town which has been long established. But that no person in the town may be allowed to set people across the river for pay, (at this place), so long as you shall allow that the benefits of this ferry hath made compensation for my private expenses, in opening a new road and making it good from this ferry to Cahokia town and making and maintaining a bridge over the river Abbe of one hundred and fifty feet in length.

Your consideration and answer to this is the request of your humble petitioner; and as an acknowledgment of the favor petitioned for if granted, I will be under the same regulations with my ferry respecting crossing passengers or property from your shore as your ferrymen are below the town; and should your people choose to cross the river in their own crafts, my landing and road shall be free to them.

And should you wish me to procure you anything that comes to market from the country on this side, I shall always be ready to serve you.

And should you have need of timber or anything that is the product of my land, it may be had at the lowest rates.

I am, sir, with due respect, your humble servant,

James Piggott.

August 15, 1797.

Although the Spanish commandant at St. Louis was anxious to have said ferry regularly carried on by said Piggott, because it was of great use to St. Louis, yet he devised a plan by which it was done without having it said that he had granted said ferry right to a *foreigner*, viz., he granted said Piggott the ferry landing below Market street, on which said Piggott then erected a small ferry house, which he occupied mostly however by one of his ferry hands, who at

[p. 66]

any time could cross foot passengers in a canoe; but when horses, &c., were crossed the platform had to be used, which required three of his men.

Neither skiffs, scows, nor yawls were then used, but the well made Indian canoe and pirogue were the water crafts used at said ferry at that early day.

The ferry tract of land which then lay between said creek and river which belonged to said Piggot, have been regularly conveyed by several deeds to the Wiggins' ferry company, and allow me to say that said company has ever been composed of honorable, energetic and liberal men, who at great expense have successfully contended against many cross currents, and greatly improved said place for the public convenience as well as their own profit.

Isaac N. Piggott.

[p. 67]

St. Louis May 21st 1866

Mr. Lyman C. Draper, Pleasant Branch P.O. Dane County Wisconsin

My Dear Sir, Being absent when your letter of 4. May arived I Did not Recievd untill the 19th.

Ondly two of the men you enquire after I was well acquainted with. Layton White of whom I can say he was a good Citize. There was nothing pecular in history that now occurs to my memory. I was more intimate with Col John Moredock. I heared him say (while at the Treaty

with the Indians held at Portage De Sioux in AD 1815)
"that in as much as the Indians had murdered his mother,
& several others of his relations, the United States might
Treate and make peace with them, but he <u>never would</u>

[p. 67¹]
he haveing already killed (14) fourteen of them, & he intended to continue the war.

    I will here inform you that his mother at the time the
Indians killer her was then called Mrs. Huff & when I git
ready to answer you letter in full, I will say more abut
Moredock; & let me request you to write to me & let me
know were I stoped the history, so that I may not travel
over the same ground when I resume.

    I am not Certain if I sent you a Copy or a Discription
of the Captans Commission given to James Piggott by the
General Assembly of Pennsylvania on the 6th. of Aprile
1776. I sepose I had it in the publised Letter to Gov.
Reynels. Be that as it may I will enclose you the original
order he Recieved on the 31. aug. 1776. you will

[p. 67²]
take care of this ancient Relic.

    I will try to resume the historicle account of the Erec-
tion of fort Jeffersom & it Defence &c as soon as you
inform me wher I stoped.

    I am truly thankful that you still have patience with
this old man & that you Can read my scrall.
Your Truly
I. N. Piggott
    P.S. The inclose original order I have heitherto re-
fused to part with, but I Send it to you. Please send me a
Copy thereof if you Can refresh me memory with anything I have writen Do send it, or any other information

you may think proper.

[p. 68]
Orders to Capt. James Piggott
<u>Sir</u>

By orders of Colls. Eniss Makay you Ar derected to March your Recruts All that you Have Enlisted under Such officer as you Can Best Spare from the Recruting Servis So as they May be at ye Ketanian on tusday the tents day of September Next. Where they are to put them Selves under ye Comand of Majr. Richard Butler. Given at Mr. Kooks August the thirtey first 1776.

Wilson Lt. Col.

To Capt. James Piggott.

[p. 68¹]
To Capt. James Piggot
on the Servis of ye united States

[p. 69]
Letter from L. C. Draper to Isaac Newton Piggott

Pheasant Branch
Dane Co: Wisconsin,
July 9th, 1866.

Isc. N. Piggott, Sen.
My Dear Sir:

I have not been as prompt as I intended, in acknowledging yr. favor of the 21st. May last, for which, & the enclosed original paper, I heartily thank you.

1st. Tell me what you can of <u>Layton White:</u> did he leave any family; had he any brothers or sisters in the Illinois country; if so, & <u>they</u> left descendants, please refer me to them. At what place & about what period, did Layton White die? What of his previous history?

[p. 69¹]

2d: Tell me all you can of Col. John Moredock's history: of his father; of a fight Moredock & others had on an Island in the Mississippi with Indians; when it happened, & the particulars? When did he die, & at what age? Can you refer me to any of his relatives?

3d. I am glad you promise to resume the Fort Jefferson history. All you sent me on that subject was yr. published letter in a Belleville paper: a single letter, & this related mostly to yr. father's Pennsylvania services. Though I have

[p. 69²]

the letter carefully filed away, I cannot just now lay my hand on it. However, I think you had not fairly got started on the Fort Jefferson history proper.

4th. If you can give me any facts about the Kaskaskia chief Ducoign, please do so.

5th. Add what you can of one Doza, a famous French hunter of yr. region.

6th. What has become of Edmund Flagg, whom I once met in St. Louis, perhaps 16 years ago?

May Heaven kindly bless you! Write soon.

Yours truly, Lyman C. Draper

I send you a pamphlet.

[p. 70]

Letter from Isaac Newton Piggott

No. 1114 Monroe Street
St. Louis Mo.
March 11st 1867

Lyman C. Draper,

Dear Sir I am just in recept of your letter of 8th. of this month. I am glad you have so much patience & perseverence. I ackowledeg my omition and if you will assist me a little I will resume my Duties. But I write this Short letter, for the Double purpose of acknowledgeing the recept of yours & asking you to refresh my memory in regard to all that I have written you, & if you have recieved my 1st letter to Gov. Reynelds Date about April 1863. published in the Bellville Advocate.

Also what part of the history of my father James Piggott his firs settlement in Illinoie & Defence of fort Jefferson &c &c. so I may not repeat unnessarily. I have sent out all the Belleville papers that Contained my first

[p. 70¹]

letter to Gov. Reynals I think you have a copy or perhaps have printed extract if so please furnish me one.

I am more than ever convined of the necessity for ancient fats to be published.

I sent you some time ago the first original order to my father when he was recruting in 1776. has you recieved it? Did I send you a Copy of his Commission dated about 6th. of Sept. 1776.

Any thing that will aid in refreshing my memory will be of use to me, if you should have any paper or pamphlet you Chose to send me tutching any of those matters. Note the parigraph you wish to direct my attention to, & I will try to furnish you a synopsis of such historical facts hitherto not Published may the Lord enable us to Do this thing Correctly.

With Due Respect I am your obt. Servt. and Chirstean brother

I. N. Piggott

P.S.   Whereas I have purchased a new Residence at which all Letters will be Delivered to me the day they reach this City if Directed Thus, or the No. is put thereon.

I. N. Piggott

No. 1114 Monroe St.

St. Louis M.O.

You will pleas excuse this hasty scrawl written after nite in hast, & tho blotted; and not revised, yet I thaught best to send it forthwith.

INP.

Commission of Capt. James Piggott

Pennsylvania SS.

April 6th 1776

LIBERTY SAFETY AND PEACE (Seal)

In Assembly

To James Piggott Esquire

We reposing especial Trust and confidence in your Patriotism, Valor, conduct, and Fidelity, Do by these presents, constitute and appoint you to be Captain of a company of foot in the Second Battalion of the Millitary Associators in the County of Westmoreland for the protection of this province against all hostile Enterprise, and for the defence of American Liberty. You are therefore carefully and dilligently to discharge the duty of a Captain of the said Associators, by doing and performing all manner of things thereto belonging. And we do strictly charge and require all officers and Soldiers, under your command to be obedient to your orders as their Captain, and you are to observe and follow such orders and direction, From time to time as you shall receive, from the assembly during their Session, and in their Recess from the present or any future committee of Safety appointed by the assembly of this province, or from your superior officers according to the Rules and Regulations for the better Government of the Millitary association in Pennsylvania and pursuant to the trust reposed in you this commission to continue in force until revoked by the assembly or by the present or any succeeding committee of safety.

Signed by order of the assembly
John Morton
Speaker

[p. 71[1]]

Captain Piggott for a while was assigned the duties of a recruiting Officer, for which he was eminently qualified, having an extensive acquaintance who knew that he had acted well his part in the independent vollenteers Co. before mentioned and ever punctual in the disbursements of public monies.

But after Gen. Washington had been driven from Long Island having lost 2000 men in the Battle of the 26th August 1776

The following order was received by Capt. Piggott, which on account of its antiquity, and its having been written in the most gloomy time of our Revolutionary Struggle; I will here transcribe and give a just exhibit thereof, on the outside of which was this directed.

"To Capt. James Piggott"

on

"The Service of the United States"
Sir/

By order of Colle. Enoss Makay you ar directed to March your Recruits all that you have Enlisted, under such officers as you can best spare from the recruiting Service, so as they may be at ye Ketanian on tuesday the

tenth day of September next where they are to put themselves under ye Command of Maj. Richard Butler.

Given at Mr. Kooks August the thirty first 1776.

Wilson Ltt. Col.

To Capt. James Piggott

[p. 72]

Will of James Piggott

To all peopel to whom this present writing shall come
of James Piggott inhabitant of the Great Run abut nine
miles from the town of Cohokia in the Ilinnoi send greeting. Know ye that I the said James Piggott for good
causes me hear unto moving and in consideration of my
being the natural father of four children born out of
Lawfull wedlock of Francis who is now my Wife: and
whos names are Mary. James. Joseph and Francis in consideration of which I have given and Granted and by
these presents do give grant and confirm unto the said
mary James Joseph and francis an equil and to each a just
and equl preportionable part of my estate rail & personal
with thoss off my two sons William and Levi, to be
devided unto each of those my children after my disseas
by my executors discretion to have and to hold all and
singular the said goods and chattels hous hold stuf or
whatever the Same may consist of from the said James
Piggott unto the said Mary James Joseph and Francis
their Heirs and assigns forever.

in Witness Whare of I the said James Piggott have set
my hand and seal this 8th Day of march one thousand
seven hundred and ninety.

James Piggott [Seal]

Alex. Dinnis
Robert Seybold
James Lemon

Marriage certificate of Jacob Judy and Elisabet Wit

Te Loran Chenberger Sousigne et Sertifie, a quil apartientra, que je vue afiché a la Maison de Ville, et a la porte de Leilise de Cahaut les afiches de pubication de Mariage Entre Jacop joudy, et Elisabet Wit, qui etoit Signe de Philipe Engel Jugr. le 29 octobre 1792

Johann lorentz Schönberger

atesté Sou Serment devent Moy pour etre juiste et veritable ce 20 Nov 1794

Philipe Engel Judg

Je Sousigne et Sertifie avoir Signé deux afipps de Bubication de Mariage, Entre Jacob Judy, et Elisabet Wit, et que personne et venue a moy, pour metha abohon donnée le presant a la prerie du pont au Compte de St Clair le 20 Nov 1794

Philipe Engel

Endorsed below: "Certificate of Marriage."

Legal actions, St. Clair Co., Ill.

Mr. Willm Biggs acting against Mr. James Piggott the 27th of oct 1795.

To Damage I have paid Michel Huff
recovered by Judgment of court,
ten Dollars   10 - 0 -
  To making 3 pair of Shoes   6 - 0 -
  Piggotts act against Biggs   16
  to corn at sundry times 15 Bushels
and a peck   15 - 2 - 5

to 9 quarts of Brandy	9 - 0 -
to 1 Bushel of potatoes	2 - 0 -
To fees on Servis as foreman	
on the Grand jury	6 - 0 - 6
	32 - 2 1
	17
	15 2 1

To all whom it doth or may Concern: Know ye that I William Biggs High Sheriff of The County of St Clair in the Territory North West of the River Ohio gave to Jas. Piggot Esqr for G ... for five days Attendce. & 60 ...

	3 0 0
to milage 2 ... 51 miles.	3 - 0 -0
	6 - 0 - 0

[p. 73³]
Sheriff Biggs act against Mr Piggot   no aconts

[p. 74]
    Processes Returnable to October Term -1796-
Wm. Arrundale vs Joseph Lacont}

	cents
Returning writ	9

Clamorgan vs Durocher}

	cents
Serving writ	37½
Committing to jail	37½
Releasing Defendant	37½
Returning writ	9

Pausanos vs Maillot}	cents
service	37½
Returning writ	9

Bailbond	<u>37½</u>

L. Lajoys vs Jos. Mandoso}	cents
Serving Summons	37½
Returning D°	<u>9</u>

J. Dumulin Esqr vs J K	
Simpson and Peter Casterland}	cents
Returning summons	<u>9</u>

Antoine Tubauq vs }	
Louis Goud and wife}	cents
serving writ	75
Return D°	<u>9</u>

To Dumulin Esq vs B	
Champler}	cents
serving writ	27
Return D°	9

An. Todd vs Grimes}	cents
Return writ	<u>9</u>

Wm. Downing vs Casbole}	cents
milage	72
Returning writ	<u>9</u>

United states vs E. Todd}	cents
serving writ	37½
Return D°	<u>9</u>

L. Lajoys vs Grondine}	cents
Milage	12
serving writ	37½

Bail Bond	37½
Returning writ	<u>9</u>
Ralal vs Piggot} sup	cents
Serving of witness	37½
Milage	12
Returning sp=	<u>9</u>
Lapage vs Velerey}	cents
serving 4 witness	50
Returning Supn.	<u>9</u>
Dawning vs Casbole}	cents
Serving 1 witness }	84½
twelve miles }	
Return supn.	<u>9</u>
Parnelle vs Martin}	cents
Serving 2 witneses	25
Return supn.	<u>9</u>
Parnelle vs Martin}	
serving 2 witness	25
Returning supn.	<u>9</u>

[p. 74¹]

October Term 1796

Parnelle vs Martin} Veture	cents
facins somg. jury	75
Parnelle vs Martin} somg.	cents
Jury	75

Lambart Lajoye vs Joseph Grondine} somg. D°	cents 75
Ranal vs Piggott} somg. D°	cents 75
Lapage vs Varey} somg. D°	75

[p. 75]
Letter from J. Edgar
Kas Kas Kias 26 May 1797

Dear Sir

I have been aplyed to by one John Bottom for to marrey him but as it is not in our County I cannot do it he beges of me to write you a few lines on that Business as he is not aquainted with you I told him you could not marry him untill he was fifteen days publickly

You remember I Spake to you concerning Mr. McGlachlans militia Right as he was not in the first but I begs of you to have him entered in the Subliment you have to make I spake to Col. William St. Clair he is with Mr. John Dumolin the two witness to the sale pleas not to forget and Oblidge

Your sincre freind
Camptt. ... Jam
J. Edgar
famialy

[p. 75¹]
James Piggot Esqr
Grand Rusins

[p. 76]
Letter from Mary J. Brock
Death of Isaac Newton Piggott.
Saint Louis June 26th / 76
Mr. Lyman C Draper
Dear Sir
your letter received sory to say Father is no <u>more</u>, he died 11th February 1874
Respectfuly
Mary J. Brock

[p. 77]
Letters from John Reynolds

Belleville 1st June 1853
Dear Sir

I had the pleasure to receive your letter yesterday, and will answer it so far as I am capable. I am sorry I can not give much of the information requested, but I may act as <u>the whetstone, if not the knife.</u>

I am glad you have spent so long a time in the search of western material, as I doubt not your time was occupied advantageously, and I am certain it was spent with honor to yourself and country.

I left East Tennessee in the year 1800, and only back to school; so I can not say personally any thing about Genl. Sevier. I saw him in Knoxville: but know nothing personally of him. I was in Congress for many years with his son from Arkansas. The family papers, I presume, are with his wife, who was a niece of Col. R. M. Johnson of Ky. Her father lives about the Little Rock, who could give you information perhaps.

I am going to East Tenn. soon and will enquire of Genl. Sevier's early life. I will write you on the subject.

I never saw Danl. Boon. I was in Genl. Howard's campaign in 1813 with his son Nathan Boon. Did you know that both Messe. Peck and T. Flint have written lives of Boon.

There is an author in Baltimore I am informed, writing the life of Genl. G. R. Clark. His nephew Col. John O'Fallan of St. Louis Mo. was raised by Clark his uncle and can give you more information, that has not been made public than any other man. This nephew in St. Louis has Genl. Clark's old war papers.

Of these pioneers you mention, Kennedy Roddie, Kelly, Outlaw White &c. I had heard much in Tennessee: but can give no facts in relation to them. Capt. Be... married a relative of my father's and I knew him personally before 1800 in Tennessee and after to his death in Illinois. He was a warm Indian fighter in early times in the mountains & ... He was born in the New River Country Va. I think Logan, and Dr. Todd of

Springfeild Ill. could give you much information of the Logans, Todds and Capt. Whitley of Ky. Whitley was with Harrison & Shelby in the campaign into Canada in 1813.

The Harps commenced their bloody career in Knox Co. Tenn. about the year 1791. I have heard my father say: that he and others went to regulate them once on Beaver Creek, where they resided. I will enquire about them, when I am in Tenn.

I know nothing of Genl. Roluson, except by the Books.

You have a great task before you, which I hope you will accomplish to your own honor, and the advantage of the public. Every thing, that can be done by me to advance your honorable enterprise, shall be performed with pleasure by your friend

John Reynolds

Mr. Lyman C. Draper

Mr. Robt Forsyth, living near St. Louis could give you much pioneer information about <u>Simon Girty</u> &c as his father was born at Detroit as you see in the "Pioneer History" 208 &c. I would respectfully suggest

[p. 77³]

to you to travel one year to obtain the information you need, if you have not already got it.

[p. 78]

Knoxville 27 June 1856

Dear Sir

I understand; that Dr. Ramsey of Knoxville has written a very full history of Tennessee, so that the information you desired of me you could get in that work. I have not seen it.

The individuals you mention in your letter I can not ascertain any thing in regard to their lives, more than a general confused legend of them. If I find any thing I will write you. I will return by Nashville. I may <u>pick</u> up some thing there.

Please write me. If I can assist you with facts of the olden time I will do so with pleasure. Excuse this <u>slip shod</u> paper, and writing; as it proceeds from your friend

John Reynolds

Mr. Dreper

P.S. If I see Dr. Ramsey I will mention you to him.

Write him for copy of his book.

[p. 78¹]
[Postmark] Knoxville Te. Jun 27   5
Mr. Draper   Hon. John Reynolds
Book Makr   Knoxville, Ten. June 27, 53.
Madison
Wiscon.

[p. 79]
Belleville 16th July 1853
Dear Sir

I was pleased to receive your interesting letter on my return from Tennessee, and am sorry I can not give you any Tennessee information worthy of your notice. I wrote you: but I see by your letter, you have Ramsey's History. I bo't a copy in Nashville. I did not find it, as it was represented to me. I saw many old pinoneers in Tenn. but their information was not interesting. By taking more time many old facts might be resuscited worthy of posterity.

I am really astonished at your labor and the fruits of it in procuring materials for your future disposition. What size, shape, or form you intend for the public I do not know: but one thing certain; you deserve great credit for your talented and energetic labors thus far; and you have my sincere prayers for your success. In my humble manner, I will think it an honor, to assist you with materials, so far as I am capable. The old documents you mention, if I can find any of the war of 1812 &c. I will send them to you with pleasure.

My Black Hawk war books I sent to John Russell Esq. of Alton Ill. at present. I will try to obtain them again and forward them to you. I think, no one knows more about that small war than I do, except

the documents themselves on matters mentioned in the documents. I kept a copy of all the orders and proceedings in the books I lent to Mr. Russell.

I am pleased, I can inform you of the residences of most of the officers engaged in that war. Genl. Atkinson was a native of North Carolina; died Jefferson Barracks, and left no heirs except a wife of the Bullit family Ky. Louisville. Genl. Henry died at New Orleans a single man; was the son of Maj. Henry of Missouri and was a mechanic, a shoe maker, A Sheriff of Sangamon County and popular man, before the war. I appointed him and Genl. Alexander of Paris Egar Co. Ill. my <u>aids de camp</u> before the Black Hawk war. Col. E. D. Taylor of Chicago was one of Henry's <u>aids</u> in the war. he could give you much information of Genl. Henry. Genl. Milton K. Alexander lives at Paris as above stated, and could give you much Black Hawk information. Col. Gabriel Jones of the B. H. War was not G. Jones of Wisconsin. The war Jones lived at Nashville Ill. an excellent citizen. Genl. Whiteside is alive near Edwardsville Madison Co. Ill. but aged and not much reollection. Col. John Dement a fine Tennesseean is in the Land office Dixon Lee Co. Ill. The Hon Z. Casey is living at Mount Vernon Ill, and is an intelligent man; was Lieut. Gov. when I was Gov. in 1830 and in Congress for 8 or 10 years.

Maj. Stillman, Hackleton and Ewing are all dead. Stillman left a family at Canton Fulton Co. Ill. In the same county Hackleton lived and died. Genl. Ewing resided mostly at Vandalia Ill. His son in law Judge Dale lives in

Greenville Bond Co. Ill. But his brother in law James W. Berry Esq. in Vandalia can give you all the information of Genl. Ewing. Genl. Semple, who was in the U.S. Senate is alive and resides on the Mississippi mouth of Piasa Creek Jersey Co. Ill. Capt. A. W. Snyder is dead. His son William H. Snyder Esq. is in this City a <u>live</u> man offering for Congress. Genl. Rasey died at Shawneetown Gallatin Co. Ill. James Caldwell can give you much information of Genl. Rasey. He resides in Shawneetown where Maj. Cochran had the fight with the Indians in the Summer of 1765.

The Hon. John A. McClermand late in Congress, resides at Jacksonville Ill. and can give you much B. H. information as he was in the war. Judge Thos. C. Browne of Galena Ill. was the Aid of Genl. Atkinson. He could inform you of facts in this matter. John A. Wakefield wrote a book on the Black Hawk war. Did you ever see it? Col. Collins lives same where in Wisconsin. Col. John J. Hardin who was killed at <u>Buena Vista</u> was an aid of Genl. Joseph Duncan in the Black Hawk war. Gov. Jos. Duncan was a Lieut at Lawee Sandusky under Craghan in 1813 at that bloody fight. Maj. McConnell of Jacksonville Ill. was in the Black Hawk war, and could

[p. 79³]

inform you much on the Subject: But my Quarter Master Judge Wm. Thomas can give you more <u>facts</u> of this war than almost any one I know. He resides at Jacksonville Ill.

There are several young Clarks in laws the sons of the brother of Genl. G. R. Clark, who can give you information of their uncle derived from their father. Col. John O. Fallon was the adopted son of Genl. Clark and had his old papers. You have them perhaps.

The Revd. Mr. Peck informed me: that there was an old man Mr. Martin in St. Louis Mo. who could unfold much pioneer information of the first Settlement of both Kentucky and Missouri.

I feel truly interested in you and your enterprise, and will do all in my humble manner to assist you. I will send you a pamphlet or picture, and altho' it is not in your ... please read it, and write me what you think of it. I have a small printing press, and a small <u>mania</u> for scribling, so that I may make an other edition of the "Pioneer" with a few sheets of my humble life added to it. I had some notion of making a small pamphlet shewing the Simila... between Mohammed and Oliver Cramwell. I have nothing on hands, and have a small wealth; no children, and this is my manner of sewing my old wild Oats.

Please write, & a little about your ... profession &c. and oblige your friend

John Reynolds

Mr. L. C. Draper

[p. 80]
Belleville 5th August 1853
Dear Sir,

I had the pleasure yesterday to recieve your letter, and feel much interest for success and general welfare. I feel as I expressed in my former letter: that it will afford me pleasure to be an humble <u>Aid de camp</u> of yours so far as I am able.

My wife has been unwell; so I have not went in person to our friend John Russell now of Alton, Ill. to regain my old military books of the Black Hawk war. So soon as I can leave home I will be in that search <u>head and ears</u>. I feel interested in the war to put the affair in ship shape before the public; as I was, like Eaneas said to Dido, a part of the transaction. Mr. Walkefeild lived in Joe Davis Co. Ill. the last I heard of him. I presume you can get the book about Galena. There are none here, that I know of. It is not great at best. I kept no files of either the Black Hawk times, or the times of which the peneer treats. Much of the facts contained in that work I recd., as the lawyers say on terms of the old men. I knew a good deal myself &c. I am sorry I can not furnish you any thing in your line. Genl. Jacob Fry is a native of Ky., took his rise in Green Co. Ill., was Sheriff then, went to the Legislature, and then Col., not Genl. in the Hawk war. He is now in Calafornia and is a good man. He was many years a canal

[p. 80¹]
commissioner on our canal. Write to Joel Manning Esq. Lockport Ill.; he will ... all about him. Let me say to you about the Black Hawk war, there is no man this side of Heaven, that can give you more information of, and concerning it than I can; and will do so; ... I refresh my memmory by my ... books, and otherwise. You use it as you ...

Col. Fry has brother living in Green Co. Ill.

I understand Genl. Rosey was of the great Rosey family ...lution. Col. James Sloo at Shawneetown Ill. or his brother Thos. Sloo at New Orleans, can give you all about the family &c. The aged Rosey at Henderson, I presume, is of the same family with our Genl. Our Illinois Brady was not ... all the Pittsburgh Brady. Our Thom lived here in Cohokia with the French, I ... before the Revolution; was Sheriff of this Co. &c. Mr. Nicholas Boismenue ... son of the Boismenue with Brady informed me of the expedition; as related in the Pioneer. I think the date is correct. I will ... the son, who lives near Illinois Town, and know more certain about the ... You can write him; as you know ... residence. This expedition was gotten up at the instance of Brady and others of the citizens of Cohokia and <u>Prairie du Pont</u>. Clark knew nothing about, I presume.

Three old men, James, Joseph and ... Lemon, reside near the post office Collinsville, Madison Co. Ill. They could tell you of their ancestors, and the Ogles ... at the battle at Wheeling, where the ... run to get the powder. The old Ogles

[p. 80²]
are dead. Dr. J. M. Peck who is now in N. York, and perhaps in the ... could tell you much about those old Lemon & Ogle affairs. Write him. The Post office near Maj. Brown is Mascoutah St. Clair Co. Ill. I think he is not of the family you mention.

Samuel Whiteside is the name of the General. Wm. B. & John D. Whiteside were brothers raised at "the old Station"; came to Illinois in 1792 so, I think, says, The Pioneer. They are cousins to Genl. Saml. W. The Genl. is alive near Edwardsville Madison Co. Ill. Both of their fathers I think fought on the right side at Kings mountain. This gives a man in the South west a title of nobility, if he wants it.

I know not scarsely any thing of P. Trammell. He lived in Boon's Lick country, and there, I think, died. Thomas C. Brown of Galena, Ill., late one of the Satn. Judges of our State, could give you all the <u>news</u> about Trammell. The Judge (Brown) is not fond of labor writing, but has good sense and was an <u>Aid</u> of Genl. Atkinson in the Hawk war. He could tell you much of the war. John A. Wakefield is in Joe Davis Co. Ill. and where his book is also. I can not say, if Duff whom the Indians killed in 1799 is one of Clark's men, or not. I could find out. One of my old friends Major John T. Lusk is alive at Edwardsville, Ill. & could tell you much about Duff, Genl. Lapey and all about the Ohio, in 1798, and for some years thereafter. His father had the ferry on the Ohio. He came to Edwardsville in 1805, and would think it a compliment from you to write him. His memory is good. Please write him. I consult him often.

One Duff and Wm. Going made salt at the saline near the Ohio in very early

[p. 80³]

times. If I publish the Pineer again; I will, I think, put a scene in it of Duff and Goings being in the hands of the soldiers & escaping &c. which are facts: but do not add ... to the credit of the parties. It was a trouble to me, and to my sense of propriety, to Steer clear of giving offence to the honest posterity of a doubtful ancestry, in my Pioneer. My nature is not malice, except forced to it. This may be boasting but, nevertheless; I think true. This trait makes all my pioneers, I fear, rather too good characters.

I read with the greatest pleasure your memoir of yourself, and appreciate that honest candor, that breathes thro it. I, in former days had some power with political men, and if I have any at present, I would be much pleased to exert it in your favor for some office, such as Stephens had to ... the ... in Spanish America. I would have influence with Genl. Dodge and son I think, and also with Genl. G. W. Janes. I will exert it for you, if an occasion occurs. I will write, at all events to Genl. Dodge. If I could see my friends for you, it would be better than letters. You will not fail to write me as often as convenient. I fear, your rligious notions and mine will not agree. I think, we aught to be more liberal and tollerent than the Calvinist creed permits us. Some of the Baptist folks are Simon pure Calvinists. Genl. S. Whiteside is a Baptist. I would be pleased, if I could ... something to aid the sale of your intended life of Boon. I am in a small paper for a short time, where we could give you notoriety in this State without cost to you.

Your friend
John Reynolds

L. C. Draper Esqr.

[p. 81]

Belleville 9th Oct 1853

Dear Sir

Before 9 A.M. to day I recd. your note of the 4th inst. and am always pleased to hear from you. Do not consider it a "bore to me to hear of your plans & hopes" &c. It is a pleasure to me and I will assist you all I can in my humble manner. Your zeal and enthusiasm are so Sincere, and laudable, on western information to publish; that I have caught some of your fire, I believe: as I am now for my amusement revising the Pioneer History of Illinois and will publish a new edition.

I believe I wrote you; that I enclosed your letter last recd. letter, except this today, to our School commissioners at Springfield with a request to write you. I will, perhaps, see them at the Cattle Fair at the Seat of Government. If so I will urge the Subject on them. They are my warm friends.

I knew intimately well <u>Mrs. Ra-</u>

[p. 81¹]

<u>chel Edgar</u>, the first wife of Genl. <u>John Edgar</u>. They both were residents of Kaskaskia in 1800, when my father arrived at that village.

This lady, so far as I recollect of her birth, was born in some of the states, perhaps, Pennsylvania. She was not French; but could speak the language to some extent. She was rather smaller than ordinary, and her person was well formed and erect. She was not robust or strong but rather weak of person but generally healthy. Kaskaskia, where she lived was always healthy. She had been well raised in fashionable society, judging from her deportment. She was exceedingly kind and benevolent to the poor. I have seen her bestowing gifts and kindness to poor squaws and their children. Her eyes were blue, and her habits and deportment were those of a lady. I cannot say any thing of her education. Her mind was ordinary: but her morals were good and ... virtue above suspicion. She was, I think, in her religion a Church

[p. 81²]
of England member. She, nor her husband, was not Catholics. She seemed to me to possess a kind of melancholy about her character, that made me suspect: but not know: that she was doing penance for some foible commited in her youth. This is not to be in print. It is entre nous. You can read French. I think she was handsome when young. When I first saw her, she was a comely matron of about 40 years old. I feel kind to her character; as she was so tender to suffering humanity. She died about 1827.

I would not be surprised; she came off with Genl. Edgar in a fit of love, and they married in cool blood afterwards. I do not know this.

I knew nothing about Maj. Hugh Beaird. He was not the brother of Maj. John Beaird. John had a brother Hugh: but he never appeared above the masses. You will see much of John Beaird in 4th vol. p. 453 Amer. State

Papers. I never heard of Mr. Obediah Terrill. I will enquire about him and write you.

[p. 81³]
I did not know either Genl. Ben. Harrison or Wm. Neely of Missouri.

I am pleased to know you are geting along with Boone. And how is your your wife in the mean time. Give my compliments to her.

Write your friend John Reynolds often.
L. C. Draper Esqr.
[Postmark] Belleville Il. Oct 10
Lyman C. Draper Esq.
Madison
Wisconsin

[p. 82]
Belleville 26th Jany. 1854
Dear Sir
I am anxious to hear from you, and I therefore write you. I hope "the silken cords" have been tied around your heart; so that evry pulsation is hard and strong for your wife. Give her my good wishes for her happiness, and such other things, as wives desire.

I am still on my scribling hobby, and had some notion to print & bind a pamphlet of the country I traveled over last fall from this place & St. Louis, Chicago, Toledo, Niagara Falls, to New York and the Crystal Palace. Now what I want you to do for me is to write me the facts of the rise, origin, and present State of Adrian, Toledo, Cleveland, Erie, Dunkkirk and Buffalo &c. This northern section of the Union is a giant, so are the Falls of Niagara, the Crystal Palace, &c. My travel was eliptic: as I came home by Baltimore, Wheeling &c. How far from

Toledo was the old English fort, that Pontiac captured? Please write me all the ancient

[p. 82¹]
doings and history of the north of your native state Ohio, some times called Oyo by "the first settlers". Where was Wayne's battle on the Maumee? Was Cleveland first occupied by the French? The trait of antiquity is still "sticking out" in me. Lower Sandusky is not far from the railroad. I traveled the railroad, so that you may know the tract about which I hope you will write me. How many souls have Toledo, Cleveland Erie &c.

I will be in Springfield for some weeks after the 9th Feby. where I would be pleased to receive your letters. The Legislature sits there.

I have a press, and if my publications are not much, they will not cost much. Like the preacher: "Poor preac... poor pay."

How comes you on with ... Danl. Boon? Please write your friend

John Reynolds

L. C. Draper Esq.

[p. 83]
Belleville 25th Feby. 1856

Dear Sir,

I have recd. many interesting papers from you and for the same you have my thanks. Your address delivered some time since to the Society was truly eloquent and classic.

I had the pleasure to enclose by mail to you a copy of "My Own Times & life" which I hope you have read. The work was more approved than I anticipated. The Black Hawk, and war of that name, are extended in the work perhaps too much.

I am now amusing myself on abridged biography published in the newspapers by chapters. I finished a sketch of <u>Genl. Clark</u>, one number of which I sent you. I am now on Bonaparte. I fear I may rant into the bombast like Abbott or Barnum on Balie Shows. It is difficult to remain on the Solid Earth when a person is writing the extraordinary exploits of either Clark or Bonaparte.

[p. 83¹]

I had some intention to write and publish a small volume of the life of <u>Genl. Clark</u>. I think it would sell gotten up in a cheap form. I urged in my last Chapter of <u>Clark</u> that a monument be erected in honor of <u>Clark</u>, and his Illinois Campaign in the Revolution, and located on Corn Island opposite Louisville Ky.

I am sorry we lost Mann Butler Esqr. He had <u>Clark</u> much at heart. Have you any documents relative to <u>Clark's</u> life in your possession? The close of his life casts a gloom over his freinds; But his youthful brilliant career will always fill a bright page in his country's history.

Our friend <u>Dr. Peck</u> is writing biography. He was sick last fall, and is yet ... health. He labors night and day. Professor John Russell of Bluff Dale Green Co. Ill. is happy amongst his books, freinds and grand children.

I know not what I may do in this mundane travel: but I can not be idle. I lectured for the first time in my life on education last week.

Please write your frend
John Reynolds

Lyman C. Draper Esq.

[p. 84]

Belleville 12th May 1856

Dear Sir

I was pleased with your kind letter, and send you all I wrote of <u>Genl. Clark</u>. I want the sketch deposited with other such documents in your archives of western history, and of course, you to use it, if worthy of your attention.

I am pleased to know, you are about to start in on the <u>General Clark,</u> and hope for your success in the performance: No doubt, the work will be hailed all over the union; as a hidden treasure bro't to light; as

[p. 84¹]

Clark was one of the greatest of the Great. How do you think of my closing scene of Clark? It is painful; our hero did not do better towards his decling days. I would think you would do good by publishing in your papers, the hint I wrote to erect a monument for him at, or near, Louisville, Ky.

I take pleasure in presenting a copy of My Times to your lady, and hope, she and you may have offspring, who will laugh over my youthful scenes.

I am at a stand what next I will turn my attention to. I can not be idle. I dislike politics

[p. 84²]

and law, and will attack some useful subject in my unpretending manner of writing. The public for sympathy, or otherwise, have given me much credit for my humble works.

I am about to publish an other edition of My Times. I think 3, or 5,000 copies will sell; as well, or better, than the first 1000. All I care for, as to money is, that they pay for the publication.

What ails your wrist? You had better commence your <u>Clark</u> soon. Time is moving on.

I have printed in a news paper an abridged life of Bonaparte which I think I will complete

[p. 84³]

and publish in a pamphlet of about 150 pages. I like the work tolerably well but we are so partial to our offspring.

One of two subjects I had a notion to attack: the history of the state of Missouri or the Pioneer Lives of western prominent men. I had some idea of <u>Genl. Clark</u> on condition, you did not undertake it: but now I resign all my pretensions to you with all my heart. What think you of the abve subjects, and which would be preferable for me. Please write me, and believe me to be to you and lady

A friend
John Reynolds

L. C. Draper Esq.

[p. 85]

Belleville 4th June 1856
Dear Sir

I send you two papers of <u>Clark on both sides</u> and hope you have commenced to put in durable and instructive history his whole eventful life. Do not delay too long your labors.

I know of but one Mr. <u>Greathouse</u> he lives in Vandalia Illinois, and is the son and nephew of two Gentlemene of Kentucky of that name.

I have rather descided to write the history of Missouri, let it turn out "a Song, or Sermon" as <u>Burns</u> says.

It is rather presumptious to reach over the great Inland sea for work.

I wish you would give your mind and documents, books &c. an examination, and see if any thing, you have, would suit my case. You have visited the patriarch, Boon's children.

Please write me what you have in store mental, or physical, in this connection and oblige your friend

John Reynolds

Lyman C, Draper Esqr.

P.S. There was 30 years since a farmer <u>Mr. Greathouse</u> in Edwards County Ill. but I presume he is dead. The Hon. Judge <u>Wilson</u> of Carmi, Ill. could give you information of this farmer <u>Greathouse</u>.

Does <u>Genl. Dodge</u> the U.S. Senator live in Madison? If so, you could see him for me.

[p. 85¹]
                    [Postmark] Belleville Ill. Jun 4
Lyman C. Draper Esqr.
Secty. Hist. Society
Madison
Wisconsin

[p. 86]
                    Belleville 15th Sept, 1856
Dear Sir

I confess, I have trespassed on your kindness in not writing you sooner: but my apology is bad health and hesitation to accept the honor confered on me to make your Annual Address. The travel to the scenes of the Black Hawk war, and to see you, is a pleasure: but the ability to make an Address, that will pass muster is the question, that is not yet settled in my mind. I beg your indulgence only a day or two more, and I will write you, yea or nay, with the friendship of a friend, let the descission turn out either way.

I am glad in the heart, to see you on the pinicle of political glory to presceve the union from the grap of fanatiscism. Those deluded people in the north are unfit for the Government of the country, while they are crazy. I am doing all in my power for the Union, by speeches and writing. Next week I will send you an article on politics from the news papers which I wrote. Illinois will elect the Buch. ticket: but it is the runing of Filmore that does much service. Buch. will get all the slave states and Pennsylvania Illinois and California.

I was sedentary for a year or so at "My Times," and the Doctors say, this

[p. 86¹]

inactivity made my liver trorpid, and the result was a bowell complaint since May last. I am weak yet: but better. If I get well, I am in for a book. I may attempt the history of Missouri. I have many "castles in the air." Some must fall without noise, or any trouble to any one, only, perhaps, to myself.

May I not ask you how you are progressing with the life of Clark? Do my friend write it. You have deservedly gained much honor and standing by your exertions for the "Historical Society," and otherwise; so your book would sell right off in my opinion.

The life of your Senator H. Dodge is eventful. A picture of it to nature would sell. It should be written after the manner of Danl. Defoe in his Robison Crusoe. <u>Dodge</u> was a pioneer born and raised on the frontiers. I think his mother was also the mother of Senator Lynn of Mo. Mrs. Lynn is, I am told, writing her husband's life. Books are being produced now like a farmer sows wheat for a crop.

If descide to attempt an Address I want you to give

me the outlines of such one; as will take at your institution.

I pray for the happiness of your lady, and self, your friend

John Reynolds

L. C. Draper Esqr.

[p. 87]

Belleville, Ill. 22nd Sept 1856

To the Hon. The Historical Society of Wisconsin

I have recieved by the friendship of your excellent and efficient corresponding secretary, <u>Lyman C. Draper</u> Esqr., the appointment to deliver the Annual Address to your Society in January next, and for which distinguished honor I tender to you my sincere gratitude, and warmest friendship.

Ever since the commencement of your Association, established, as the Smithsonian Institute at Washington City, for "the Increase and Diffusion of Knowledge amongst men", I have taken the liveliest interest in it, and am happy to say: that your Society has in its present usefulness, and future prospects, surpassed the anticipations of its warmest friends. It stands proudly eminent in the front ranks of this class of institutions in the Mississippi valley, and bids feir in a few years, to rival any in the Union. This is the more surprising; as the site, where this institution stands, and the whole country around it, were very recently occupied by the savages, and only within a few years reclaimed to civilization, and literature. The exertion of the same talents and energies, that has within such short time, produced such wonders in the general progress of the west, has also reached this institution, and made it the Queen of science in the valley of the Mississippi.

Many of the most scientific and distinguished characters throughout the country are members of this association, and connected

[p. 87¹]
with it. This will guarranty the continu... of the high standing and character already enjoyed by the institution, and its future usefulness. To continue, and still advance society in all its branches, many individuals better qualified and capable to deliver the Annual Address than I am, may easily ... procured. On this ground alone, that others will do more honor and service to the institution than I can, that I most respectfully decline the appointment, hoping and beseeching the public to continue their patronage to this society.

I remain with liveliest sentiments of respect and esteem

Your friend
John Reynolds

[p. 88]
Belleville 16th Nov. 1856
Dear Friend

I am in the enjoyment of peace and happiness, and sincerely hope you taste the same blessings.

We have gained Illinois for the Democracy; but lost minor affairs. The Legislature is with us. I got so, I could stand for hours on the stumps, and I did so. I discovered: that position changes the force and effect of addresses: I told the masses the truth: that I was steping from time to eternity, speaking almost from the grave, and imploring the preservation of the union from the hands of the fanatics. In former days I spoke frequently, when I was a candidate myself and it did not effect so much; as in this last campaign.

I am exceedingly well pleased, you sent me the volume, the Report of your Society, and for the same, you have my sincere thanks. I have read with pleasure the tales of olden times, related by many; whom I know well. I was well acquainted with Messrs. <u>Shaw, Parkison, Lockwood</u> and others who wrote for your book.

You may rest assured: that the truth of history as to the termination of the Black Hawk war, is not sustained by the historians of the Wisconsin soldiers. I met the Illinois army at Rock Island, as they returned from the Bad Axe battle, and conversed with them; saw <u>Genl. Henry Cols. Fry, Jones</u>, Major <u>McConnell</u>, and others have writen me, so that I Sincerely believe: that the narration of that event in "My Times" will stand the test of time, and the

[p. 88¹]
scrutiny of truth. Many hunderds still live in Illinois, who were in the campaign in question and can and will speak the truth, if called on. I have a long narrative manuscript from Maj. McConnell; as to the details of the case. I see nothing in the statements of Col. Bracken, Parkison, or others that would authorise me to change a line in my narrative of the <u>finale</u> of the Black Hawk war.

And the same as to the cause of the Winnebagoe disturbance in 1827. The poor Indians had no idea of a general war with the Government. I anticipated some contradiction; as to the cause of the war: but I have heard, as yet, none. Indians did no injury after they obtained their squaws.

I am glad you are ... on your history of Genl. Clark, and hope to see it in a short time. I know not what I will do. I can not be idle but it is a great labor to obtain material for the Missouri history. ... writing is nothing to the other. I know ... of the times of Missouri myself, which a ... on, and near, the Missisippi, since 1800: but it would require much physical, as well as mental, labor to pile up the materials for the volume. I am not yet well. When I get strong, I may ... the work lighter. I had some notion to publish a pamphlet to separate church and state, and to drive back the spirit of Abolitionism. Of this work I am not descided. Always, I sincerely pray for the happiness of you and family and in ... same spirit, I sign myself your freind

John Reynolds

L. C. Draper Esqr.

[p. 89]

Belleville 10th Dec. 1856

Dear Sir,

I send you a letter of our friend Professor <u>Russell</u> to show you what a scolding he gave me, and for your to see what chaste and elegant composition he deals in, even when jesting with his friend. Please return it in your next; as it is private.

I had the pleasure to recieve your kind letter and the County of Dade, and for which you have my thanks.

A lawyer Mr. <u>Greathouse</u> resides in Vandalia Ill. who is the only one of that family, that lives in the state that I know.

I am glad to see you in such a fever to save the union from the hands of the fanatics. I think, I will give the Church and state a small blast; that may do both service.

It is exceedingly importinte; that the Prest. Elect should appoint a strong cabinet. I would be pleased; you would get my cabinet for the Prest. in your paper as follows. Marcy for secty. of State <u>Cass</u> for the Treesury,

Choat of Massa. Atto. Genl. <u>Robt. J. Walker</u> of Mis. Post
Mast. Genl. <u>Hunter</u> of Va. Secty. of the Navy, and

[p. 89¹]
and H. Cobb of Geo. Secty. of War. I know not a better
man for the Interior than Phelps of Mo. I dislike to hear
of Appleton and Tenney named for large stations. These
little men of one horse power will not do.

Please give your lady my best respects, and the Same
to yourself from your friend

John Reynolds

Lyman C. Draper
[Postmark] Belleville Ill. Dec 10
Lyman C. Draper Esqr.
Secty. Hist.. Socty.
Madison, Border of Symms' Walk
Wisconsin
Ice and snow and the
Cars stoped

[p. 90]

Belleville 1st. Dec. 1859

Dear Friend

I am always pleased to hear from you and in the same
spirit of good and friendly feeling to you I write you.

I have been doing little or nothing for the last year, or
more, and I am at times studying "masterly inactivity," as
Mr. Calhoun expressed it. I do not feel much ambition to
try to do any thing for the public, more than ordinary.
We are about even in our accounts, and I think, both sides
are rather disposed to permit our relations to stand still,
between me and the public. If I publish any more works,
I will consider them <u>dead born</u>; and do it for my own
amusement, and passtime.

Under this view of myself I have little confidence in any work I might publish being in merit up to the standard of bare mediocrity.

Yet I have an <u>itching</u> to write the biography of Genl. G R. Clark. If I did I would visit the place in Kentucky of his long residence and death to

[p. 90¹]
obtain original materials. I tryed to rouse the people to erect a monument to his memory: but the public mind would not be excited on the occasion, as least, by me.

I have an excellent printing office: so I could publish without great expense: but I owe the public nothing.

I will try to hunt up the letter of <u>Dr. Peck</u> you mention and send it to you.

It is strange you are a Douglas man; as that man has all over the union destroyed the Democratic party. His repeal of the Missouri compromise gave the Abolitionist foothold, and his hostility to the Dred Scott aught to kill him with all Democrats.

I am sorry you were not selected in the school service; but I was much more awfully behind, than you; when I was on the Nat. Dem. tickett in 1858.

Please write me often, and say, if you still possess much matter of <u>Genl. Clark</u>.

Your friend
John Reynolds

L. C. Draper Esqr.

[p. 91]
Belleville 11th Oct. 1862
Dear Friend

Your letter was to me, producing as much: pleasure as the sounding the trumpet of Gabriel does to persons, who have passed <u>with success</u>, "through this vale of tears". You labor too long and too much on the life of <u>Clark</u>. But I will give you some of the information desired in your letter.

In your first you request information of some of the soldiers of Clark. <u>Ben. Bond</u> of Carlyle Ill. is the near connection of the soldier <u>Bond</u>, and is writing a history of the family. He will give you the information asked for.

The Revd. <u>James Lemen</u> a relative of the Ogle family can tell you all about Judge Biggs, the Ogles and Rutherford.

Mr. <u>Leman</u> is the relative also of Judge <u>Biggs</u>. Mr. <u>Leman's</u> Post Office is Collinsville Madison Co. Ill.

<u>Newton Piggott</u> is the son of Capt. Piggott. He is also an

[p. 91[1]]

author and lives in St. Louis Mo. He will be pleased to write to you.

Mr. Hay had brothers and sisters in Upper Canad. His son <u>Andrew Hay</u> of this City will give you information of the family.

<u>Richard Bradsby</u> of Lebanon St. Clair Co. Ill. is the near relative of <u>Tom Higgins</u> and can tell all about the fight.

<u>Mrs. Jarrot</u> of St. Louis Mo. can tell you much about <u>John B. Point Sable</u>. He lived at Peoria and died on the ground where Chicago now stands. He came from St. Domingo and was <u>a mix</u> of the white and black man. <u>Peter Menard</u> of Tazewell Co. Ill. can tell you all about the the half breed Indian chief <u>DuCoign</u>. I think Mr. <u>Greathouse</u> still resides in Vandalia Ill. <u>Jesse Morrison</u> resides in Galena Ill. and is of the old stock of the family. I fear I can not find Dr. ... letter. If I do I will send it to

you.

Thus above I send you some information you requested. I retain your letter to find out the rest you desire.

I am amusing myself in writing

[p. 91²]
a pamphlet to improve & pacify religion. I know not if I will print it. I have attempted to abolish the idea of a special Providence, a regeneration the especial Grace of the Lord, and such other church trimmings, as do not exist in my opinion.

I believe much of the doings in churches are formalities and ceremonies that do not aid religion in the sight of Heaven. These wonders, miracles &c in religion are mostly gotten up by the clergy to gull people. I believe, a man cannot be happy without pure religion from the Bible governs his actions thro' life.

Did you ever reflect on the religious fanatiscism of the churches. I belive it was the errors of the churches that mostly caused the present horrible condition of our country.

I am not in fulle health; and have not robust vigor in my person. Your friend

John Reynolds
L. C. Draper Esqr.

[p. 91³]
[Postmark] Belleville Ill. Oct
Lyman C. Draper Esq.
The Captain General
of the Hist. Society
Madison   Wis.

Belleville 8th Nov. 1862

Friend Draper,

I was myself intimately acquainted with Col. John Moredock from the year 1802 until his death. I saw him shoot, play cards for money, dance and play on the violin. He was generally the largest man mentally in any crowd of pioneers in which he appeared. Nature did much for him and he pulled back against himself all his life. He was large and possessed much manly beauty. I was with him in a campaign to the head of Peoria Lake in the fall of 1812. He was a Major and I a private. He was an excellent deer and bear hunter, and I was not. Since I wrote my first letter to you, I went and with the relatives of Moredock Mssrs. Ben. Scott and Wm. Arundale. Their Post office is O'Fallan's station St. Clair Co. Ill. Mrs. C. McLaughtin may know something of him. Her P.O. is Vandalia, so may Ben. Bond ...

I did not see Harper's Monthly, and I have none of the work as I know of. Wm. H. Brown Esq. The Big Dady of the Hist. Society at Chicago, or Judge Lockwood at Aurora, or Judge Hall at Cin-

cinnatti, O, can give you information of the works of Hall.

Genl. Lacy died, I think, on the Kentucky side of the Ohio river, and Judge Dunn of Dodgeville Wis. perhaps can give you information of Genl. Lacy.

I know nothing of Trommell in Missouri. He moved there, and I think Genl. Dodge, Ex-senator, might know some thing of him.

I saw Wetzell's character in De Haas' history of the Wheeling warriors: but know him not.

I know nothing of <u>Tallenash</u> or <u>Neeley</u> of Cape Girardeau.

Genl. <u>Dodge</u> might know the last two named men in Mo.

As to <u>Tom. Brady</u> write Lawyer Brackett of Cahokia Ill. and to his grandmother <u>Mrs. Julia Jarrot</u> St. Louis Mo. <u>Mr. Brackett</u> will ... for two good old relatives of <u>Brady</u> Messr. <u>Isadore Le Compt</u> and his brother <u>Louis.</u> They may give you <u>Tom's</u> Pedigree.

The Lord sent us <u>sunshine</u> the late elections. We must drive back the Abolitionists into the same hole; they came out of.

I wish you a large family and grandchildren. Your friend

John Reynolds

L. C. Draper Esqr.

P.S. <u>R. Bradsby</u> of Belleville <u>pro hae vid</u> is a near relative of <u>Tom Higgins</u> and knows some thing not in print.

[p. 93]

Belleville 1st Feby. 1863

Dear Friend:

Before I answer your letter, permit me to ask you, if you believe going into a church, being regenerated and the sins wiped off, as some times asserted, does the person obtaining the favor any service; or is there any reality in it.

I write the above, as I see almost all the Protestent church members are strong Abolitionists willing and anxious to carry the present war to the ruin of the country. These people commenced the war, and have commited a sin, that they can not wipe off by any blood, except their own.

I knew <u>Layton White</u>. He was an old single man, when I knew him in 1807- or '8. He was a harmless innocent middle sized man without talents and lived on the charity of the pioneers. I understood he had been with <u>Clark</u>, and on that account and other merits the people respected him. I think he has a place in the upper story.

I think you had better write Mrs. <u>Julia Jarrot</u> of St. Louis Mo. in care of her son in law <u>Mr. Tellman</u> in the place of <u>Mr. Brackett</u>.

[p. 93¹]

This old lady is the grandmother of <u>Mr. Brackett</u> and is intelligent and reliable. She was born in Ste. Genveive, has resided in Illinois, & now lives in St. Louis. She is replete with pioneer information.

Mr. <u>I. Newton Piggot</u> is now a lawyer, a land trader and was once a Methodist preacher. He has a good mind — memory, and I think may be relied on. He has of course human frailties: but his statements ... history are reliable.

Mr. <u>Bradsby</u> the near relative of Tom Higgins resides nearby in this city: but dislike writing. He has an intelligent son in law in town <u>Dr. Perryman</u> perhaps, would undertake the revision of the sketch of Higgins. I have urged on the public such histories, and others as <u>Higgin's</u> and it has done no good so far as I discover. I have rather ... operations on the account of doing no good.

You deserve imm... credit, and the thanks of the publick for your unceasing ambition to do mankind a service. It is for you and not for the public that I write you. God bless you. I would be happy to see you.

Your friend
John Reynolds

L. C. Draper Esq.

Belleville 18th Feby. 1863.

Dear Friend

I had the pleasure to receive your letter of the 9th inst. and write you.

I will say one word as to the ... war, that is killing its thousands, and destroying the country. I am for peace by two methods. The first and the best is a return to the union, and if that cannot be effected in peace, Let the south be an Independent Government. The northern Puritans will keep this war up for years if the people do not put it down. If the yankee states would be willing to secede I would be glad of it. Let them go. They made the war.

The Revd. James Lemen Post office collinsvill Madison Co. Ill. can give you all about Moredock's fighting the Indians &c. The killing was before 1801. I thing Mr. Leman can tell you all about it. Mrs. Jarrot might know of it also.

John T. Lusk died recently in Edwardsville Madison Co. His sons reside there. His father had the ferry across the Ohio in 1800.

Thomas C. Brown Judge Brown died at California within two months.

Genl. Samuel Whiteside is alive. He dined with me last summer. He lives in Christian county Ill. with his children but his office I do not know. Write to his nethew James Whiteside Troy Madison Co. He will inform you where his uncle lives. The Genl. is healthy and his memory good. I know nothing ... G. W. Brown or Big Joe Sogsto... The last may have been killed in the frays on the Ohio river some years ago in Pope Co. See Ill. Statute laws in Sam Senty's office on the Ohio Regulators. I am almost related to <u>George Hendicks</u>. He was captured by the Indians in some of the States and lived with them some time. He left them, married and died in the American Bottom about the year 1797. His children several of them live in this country. I believe his wife is living.

<u>John H. Wilderman</u>. I spoke to Wilderman and he promised to write yo if you desire it. Belleville is his post office.

There were two <u>Duffs.</u> One was <u>Moredocks</u> step father, and other was in <u>Clark's</u> army. Mrs. <u>McRoberts</u> in Waterloo Ill. could tell you much. Write her about <u>Hendicks</u>. Your friend

John Reynolds

L. C. Draper Esq.

[p. 95]

Post marked "Decatur Ill" March 28 - '64."

Friend Draper

Please critisise <u>John Kelly</u> I send you. I want you to be just in your review of the pamphlet: but I crie it thunder, if it deserves it. Send your letter to me at this place, as I may be some time with my wife to the Dr. here.

I am old 76 years, sick, and aging with my country.

26th March 1864

Your friend

John Reynolds

If John Kelly be not fit for the eyes of the <u>Liberati</u> put it in the fire

[p. 96]

Belleville 16 April 1865

Dear Friend

I live an humble <u>Otium cum dignitate</u>, as the Romans had it. I do not eat birds' tongues, or bird's nest soup. I eat often corn bread and bacon with coffee that will almost float an iron wedge.

I am rather inclinded to a national religion, as that would keep down all sects like the Mormons, that had no sense, or philosophy in poligimy.

My church is composed of three pillars, The Lord The Bible, and myself. I am

[p. 96¹]
an unworthy member: but I hope to be better.

I am sorry, that Lincoln & Co. are killed. I fear that misfortune may retard the peace.

Your friend
John Reynolds

L. C. Draper Esqr.

[p. 97]
Letter from T. L. Reynolds

Belleville Ills.
Nov. 4th 65

L. C. Draper Esq.
Madison Wis
Dr Sir:

Yours to <u>Gov Reynolds</u> Sadie my Aunt I have just opend. I would of answered it sooner, but have been very busy. I am very sorry to inform you <u>Mrs Reynolds</u> is dead also. She died six weeks after the Govs death, with Three cencers on her

[p. 97¹]
breast. Gov Reynolds library was all sold Ths day week ago so I do not know any thing of his papers. If I did know of any you wish I will send them to you.

Truly yours
T. L. Reynolds
Box 105

[p. 98]
Letters from P. Menard
Tremont Novbr 12th 1862

D Sir

Your favour of y the 16 ..., was recevd. here, a few days after it was written. At that time I had proprossd to go to Kaskaskia where I will procure more information of those two individuals Mentiond in your letter. My Sister Mrs. Maxwell, from whom if I Expected to get a true history of <u>John Edgar</u> died on the 8 Ultmo. As for <u>Jean Buples Decoigne</u> I was quite a boy at the time of his death yet I remember him well. His Father I think was a French Canadian and his mother was of the Kaskaskia tribe. Atho he dressd in the Indian Stile yet his manners & deportment was that of a French man. His hight about five Seven inches. Rather corpulent, at least in his old days. I have been told by my Father who knew him when he was a yong man that he was an Extraordary man as a hunter, & ran foot races, in which he never was Excelld. His practice, when a yong man

[p. 98²]
he was in the habit and this to emulate, his young man to run up a hill about one hundred fifty yards. it was a perfect Steaple chase as ther were no road to follow. The one who reachd the top of the hill first, was Entitled to some small booty, altho' he could out run them, he always mangd to be behind, his objet was Encairje them. There a bett made of one hundred Dollars, that he could kill more Deer than the famous & Extrordinary hunter

Alexi Doza. They return the same Evening. Decoign had Sixteen Buck Skins, & Doza had Twenty booth buck & doe Skins, but mostly doe, but the Understanding was buck & not doe, so decoigne won the bet. He was braght to court once for a Small debt of some year Standing. He ask the judge what, they wanted With him. The judge Explen to him the nature of the obligation, that he was Endeptd. for so much, & ought to be dischad. long time. In great Estonishment he put his hand on Mouth, with a great Exclamation, Why us Indians after Seven years all debts are forgotten. As the court had no jurisdiction; he being an Indian

[p. 98³]
had two wives. by the first had two daghtors by his Secnd wife who was part French, he had 2 boys one Lewis Jefferson suceded him as Chief. He was a fine looking & quite intelligent. His Brother Jean Baptiste was the best made that my eyes ever beheld. He was about six high, very white, hair long a warring, & as black as jet, but a most consunnate Drunkard.

Genl. John Edgar was a british Subject, during the ... time. He cumnded a vessel on lake Erie pending the Strugle he turn himself vessel & all, to the American Cause & during the war, he distingishd as an active sop-erter of the american cause. After peace was concluded, he & his wife both from the north of Irland, were to Kaskaskia. Old Mrs Edgar, was a very amiable Lady. She died regretted by all the French people of Kaskaskia. Elisa Stephen, his secnd wife and Subsequently the wife of Pascal the Editor of the St. Louis Republican. She was thirteen years old when she married the old Com, he being 78. The late Gov. Bond & myself with great many followers gave the happy pair a complete Chivaoree, a treat & a ball followd. He was a good man with some black Strips. He was too greedy for land, & if you will look at the American State paper, you will see perjury ...

I will be in Kaskaskia, in few days perhaps you may hear from again

Respully yurs

P. Menard

[p. 98¹]

NB. Geat Many years Ego Judge Breese & my mole John Menard were about to write the life of Alexi Doza but from some Cause, it was dropd. onley perhaps, that he was than alive. As a hunter and a trapper, he never had his equal. If you feel disposed to give Alexi, a small chapter can Furnish some incidents, which will ... your readers doubt but nevertheless true

December 30th / 62 After answering your letter I thought I would go to Kaskaskia, & ... more information but owing to Sickness in my family I have been compelld to stay at home. I Expect to See my Brother Edmond in Springfield, as he is Member of the Legislature. As he posseses a Store Legers & earley Settlement, he probably can give more accurate information, than any other. Shuld put me in possession of aything new I will write.

[p. 99]

[Tremont, Tazewell Co: Ills. Dec. 18th 1863.]

D Sir:

I have reed yours of _____ infering Unless I furnshd. you a Scetch of Alexi Daza you would b Compell, to Leave it out. If I did not furnishd. it Ere now, it was owing to the fact, you in one of your letter promisd., that you would Come down & see me, and indeed, I had enterteind the hope untill recently that you would come, and partake for a few days the Hospitality of an Illinois farmer. I have no doubt if I had seen you, face to face, I could have made a better biographey by some of your Sojestions than I can rite it down.

Doza was born about the year 1760 at Kaskaskia, Mo. under French rule and of French Parents. In those days aducation, was not attainable unless childrens were sent to the States; so the youth of those days were deprivd. of what we in these days might call a blessing. To them it was no great privation, as the most them, had to live by hunting. Easy work, as they were no inducement to make a god of money, all they care for was to get a few Spanish Dollars

[p. 99¹]
dress themselves tolerably, decentley, go to Ball dance & be merry, was the hight of their ambition. He marred. abut the year 90 to a Miss de Monbrun. It seem from this, Even in those days, there were nobles as the word (de) indicates it. I knew Mrs. Doza well. She by some means, had reced a partial Education, She was truley emphatially an amiable Lady having the greatest Solisitude for the Well-being of her children, consisting of two Boys & two girls. The only sarvivng on is his son Lexi, who is quite feeble.

How to begin with the Explout of this Extriordinay Hunter, I know not. In the absence of a true cronology as regard dates, I am redud. to the necessity, to make a Jumble of it.

I shall, open, of his Exploit, & winng a bet of 100 buck skins. Zada & Lachapelle, were out on a huntng Expedition in conpaney with Seven Lodges or Weequeeun, they were of the Kaskie tribe, Except one, a Keecapoo, who had married a Kaskaska Squaw. He was lookd upon as the greatest hunter of the day among the Copper skins.

[p. 99²]

Doza had the reputation of being an nonsuch in that department. As the county from Kaskia to Vincene op th Wabash was a vast plain, where game of all sort abouded. They were about 80 mils from Kaska, on good hunting grond, when Lachapelle, proposd. to bet his fine horse that Alexi. could beat any red skin, that ever walk the earth. A poney purse, of 100 buck Skins were made up and the day namd. when the Hunt, was to take place. no one, on that occasion was to leave, his Lodge Except the two hunters, Doza & Arrerias. On the apointed day, the Indian was off before day indeed several Shots, were heard at the camp before Lexi could be inducd. to go out. Lachapelle who had made the bet urgd. him, to be off. Doza told him not to be uneasy, but make him a cup of coffee. Lachapelle remonstrated as it would prolong the time, as the Indian, had already Shot two or thre times. Lexi, insisted, on his cup of coffee and he would not budge unless he had his coffee. No time was lost, in getting, the coffee ready.

He mounted, his horse, Spurd him off

[p. 99³]

... After he gone, they could for a good while hear the Eco of the two rifles. in the course of two or three hours Doza returnd with Seven skins seven tongues, and the half of the seven Deer he had killd. and deposited, the half of the seven Deers, at the Door of Each Lodge and retrnd to his ouse, and stretch himself on his palet. Lechapelle ask him, what he ment. He told him, he ment, he wanted another cup of coffee which was soon prepared. He than told Lachapelle to go and unsaddle his and let him go. Lachapelle remonstrated & told him he should do no such thing, but he must go out again. Doza told him, he should not so this put an end to any farther urgency, to the great chagren of Lachapelle who was already mornig his loss, for he knew the Indian would reten, with a greater number of Skins. so he did, as he brughe Twenty Skins. this was a damper on Lachapelle as one may well Emagin. Each one claming, he had won the the bet one with seven Skins & the other with Twenty. Motoscannia the cheefe call a council, to decide the controversey. The Indian told them, there were Twenty Skins, he no more today. Doza got up, and calling the chief by name & told him that he knew they were hungry and distriboted to to each lodge half of a Deer to fill theer belley, when many of then were yet asleep, that was he had to say. The old chief, after cusultng with the others decided, that Lechapelle had won the bet, and assigne for reason that when very hungry that Doza had taken pitty on them; that the sun had scarceley crept above the

[p. 99⁴]
above the trees, when he brought to Each his breakfast and that they farther must thank the great Spirit for stopping him as he did for had he hunted all day there was no question but he would have killd. all the Deer. This so mortified Indian, he paid his bet, went off on the Spur of the moment & never return to Kaskaskia. This I hold from Doza & Lachapelle. About this time Boffelows were nemeras in than vast Peraries, in fact the Inhabitants of the French Villages lived pretty much on Deer & Buffelows. He on one occasion, in company with Pierre Richard wen out on what is call grand Perarie. Spying a large drove of Buffelow, he observd. to Richard that he

would get ½ Dozen of them fine cows before he quite them. He Started afoot in pursiut. after persung them half the day he kill Eight. This was Counted a great feat, by the Indians who were Jelous of him so much so, that Walkshingaw a Brother in Law of Decoigne Complain to Genral Harrisson then in Vincenne, to prohibit him to hunt Except within a certain circuit around Kaskaskie. To please the Indian, the order was given to conscribe his huntig ground

[p. 99⁵]

within nine miles of Kaskaskie, which compell him to resort to some other mode of Making living. He got the contract to carrey the Mail from Kaskia to Vincennes twice a Month. This he perform for the Spece of two years when a singular incident unexpected to him occurd. which put an End to his Mail Carring. Gov. Harisson, having call, a council, of the Various Tribes, inhabating the than Territory of Ms. to Vincennes to a treaty. Among those present were the Kaskaskie, Weas Piankee-shews, Keekapoo & others. After the treaty the Gov. told them he was going to Kaskaskie, & St Louis & would be glad of their conpaney. The firt day went about Twenty Miles, Camp earley. Game plenty. This was in the fall when it is thought, the Deer hides heavely. The Gov told, the interpreter, to tell his children, he Should like, to have some Fresh Vennison for supper. Severels of the young men went out, and return, at night without having killd. any thing. The Gov full of Joke, told them he was truley sorrey, as he was anxtiues, and Expected, to eat Venni-son, that night & had to go to bed on an empty stomach.

[p. 99⁶]
One of the Chief told the Gov he was Equally sorrey, and

fully felt the great privation to which he as well as they were subjected to. But his Father was not aquanted with the cuning of the Deer, he would tell his Father that in this Moon, the Deer buried themselves in the ground & that was the reason Why his young men, could not give him any Venison, for his supper. The next day at noon, the Gov observd. to M Tousin Dubois he flatterd himself that he would be abondanley supplied, with Vennison, and it was for the firt time in his life, he had heard that the Deers hide themselves, under ground. Dubois told the Gov. he knew, a man, in the Company that Could unburrey them, and furnish him with venison for his Supper, and with his permission, he would send him ahead the next day and he had no doubt he would kill enugh to supply the whole Camp. Doza Doza, at protested, as he had been prohibited. This was arranged, & he selected, a long rifle, belonging to a Keekapoo chief, and about three o'clock he spurd his pacing poney — soon out of sight. They were to meet, & camp, at the <u>Beaverhole</u> a noted camping grond.

[p. 99⁷]

About sun set, the Gov and his retinu arrivd. at the designated place, and there to their astonishment found the man who could unburrey those animals that the Indians in their supperstitin, beleivd could not be found. He had kill a very large Buck a fat Doe & her fon. He told the Gov he might now feed his children, and all he ask, and that as favour, for the Gov to rovoke, his order so he might again be permitted, to hunt wherever, he choose. The Gov had forgotten, that he had once restricted him, within the bounds of nine miles. He drew a peice of paper from his Port follio, and on a Stump revokd his order and a general permit to hunt Everywhere within his Jurisdiction. At the time Galeopolis was Settled by the French, Doza was sent, once & some time twice a year, to carey letters to Pittsburg % agents, for goods to supply Kaskaskie St Louis which were Shipd from Pittsburgh. Evry mile he travelled, was beset with denger as the Indians in those days were waging war so he had to walk cautiousley. He told me he genrally travel late at night and earley in the moring, and lay by in day time, when he supposd there was danger he followd this business for several year. Nothing in these voyages happen worthey of note, if we except, a little incident which occurd near Galipolis. He was out one day with some green horne Frenchmen. He all at once Spied, some game belive bufflow. He ran ahead

[p. 99⁸]

in bending posture, & turning his head towards them, and with his hand becond. for them to remain where, they were. they became quite frighten, as they did not understand his movements they thinking he was after Indians. They would Exclaim a <u>Mon Dieu</u> nous somme finis — O God were done, and would holler, at the hight of their voices ce sont les Indiens, quel cruel sons nous allons perir. Doza would occasionaly turn rond, and with his two hands, becon them to reman quiet. This put in a perfect State trepidatin. they could Stand no longer, turing their faces towards Galipolis. Doza told me they became invisible, in less than no time, arriving at home out of breath, and reported Doza in pursuit of the Indians. Doza use to laugh immoderateley, when telling the fright of those men, and would make others laugh as he was a perfect meemiek. In 1822, I went on the head of the Wabash to induce a party of Dellewars to cross the Missisipie. My guide, was Daza, and my interporetor

was Capt. Tunis, a Dellewere chief. As we tented out
Every night he use to regale us with some fine Storys,
som not fit to put on paper but very good, to tell, he was
good... like Abraham our present Monarch, full of Anac-
dotes. One night, I reminded him, of a certain fon who
had spoken, to him, once, and was to Speak again at the
end of Seven years. Many Credulous people beleeved it
would be so, and the fon would certainly Speek again &
he Doza, had told them, he had consulted the Rev Mr.
Olivier, a man whom Every body reverd & Esteemd and
liked, for he was one acording to to God's own heart.
Hell, said he to me I went out one day in the pint, and
saw a fon feeding in a pond on moss. I shot, at him seven
time, he turn his head towards me eating moss, hence the
Storey of the Speeking fon, he would some time Sketch.

I think, I gave you, in Speeking Decoigne's huntig
match in which occasion Decoigne, killd 16 Bucks, &
Doza 20, moseley Does both claiming the bet. He and
Antoine Lachapelle went out one day about ten miles
from Kaskia

[p. 99¹⁰]

and return at night, with 96 Skins, Doza killd & Lachapelle Skind. One might be dispos to discredit, this, Storey,
it is nevertheless true, for maney of the old Settlers, told
me it was so. As a trapper he could not be Excelld. I
have knom him, to catch beavers & otters, in the Kaskaskie River, when no one Else would attempt it, for they
knu it would be lost time. His beaver bait, was conpo. of
ingredients that no one Else knew. In 1809 when a companey was form in St Louis, composd. of Pierre Chateu
Sr Augustus Chateau Manuel Lesa Willm Morisson,
Ruben Lewis, my Father, and perhaps one or two more,

Doza, & severals others were employd as hunters, & trappers, and were to Share in the profits, they getting, one half of the beavers, they caught. That, he was unfortunate during an absence of three years, was not his fault, but we must attribute to fate, or Extrem bad luck it could not be from bad management, as no one, more vigilant & carefull, Erey Step he took.

In whatever he undertook he let no one in his Secrets, Except some confidential friend his Master Genious. in the deplomacy of beaver & otter traping bear killing. Racoon catching and annihela all kind of vermints, he could no be Excelled. He had traped beaver & otters to the Amont of Several thousands Dollars, Securd. as he supposed in two Excellent Caché but the wileley Blackfeet always, on the ..., and fully aware of there hiding places, were constantly on the hunt & discovery, of those Caches. When the unfortunate George Drouillard, and the four young Shawnees — five as brave men as ever drew a bead — according to Doza's Statement as told, to me, on maney Occasion, they were attact, by as he Suppose from 100 to 200 Black-feets George & the Shawnee difended themslves, bhind small trees — too small, as he says, to hide their bodies. He think they must have fought four hours in his place of obuservation, which was about one mile from the Scene of conflict. That the attacking party, must have lost in killed, no less than Twety five. He with, another, Shawnee boy, traveld. all that night. On the third day, they arrivd. at the fort and annouced the sad catestrophey. The next day a party for 80 men detail, in persuit, Doza & the Shawnee boy as guides. They fonds the bodies of those unfortunate, brave men, cut into Mincepie.

After, gathering, what was left, of George and his brave, conpanin, they performd the last right that men owes to men, by depositing in Mother earth with sorrow & grief the remeins of their frind and conpanio, Away from frieds & relative. No one can realize, the death, of a darling boy, Except, the Mother, who gave suck, & a Father who bestow, his paternal care on a beloved Boy. To return to Doza, as his Cache, was only half a day traveling, from the Scene of conflict, the companey, went on with him, to the place where he had securd. as he supposd. his beaver Skins. Here, he was disappointed, as the same party, who had killd. George Droulleard had found his cache, leaving Lexi. to Sorrow for his loss. After this Epoch, he became as the French says, <u>insousiant</u>, so after an absence of three years, he return, home as poor as he had started. I will go back, and prior, to his trip, up the Missouri, & relate the following incidents which may have occured and are to be receiv, with

some degree of doubt, as they are not Corrobreted, by others. I would here remark that Doza, certainly, a very Extraordinary Man would when he had chance make himselfe braver, than he naturally was, for his prowess was always doubted by those who knew him best. Some sixty years Ego, the Keekapoo Sacks & foxes, were wageing war aganst, the Kaskakie tribe, frequently meking incursions on on these peaceble & good Indians. By the way of degression, from my Subject, I would State, her the attack on the Kaskaskias, while Canping on Big Gullom, some thirty miles east of Kaskaskie, by party Keekopoos nunberng, some 3 to 400 warriors. The attack was made before day the Kaskaskias could not have been, more than 150 men. Taken by surprise they fought Untill, day, when they had to subcomb, to superior force. Men women & children, fare all alike, indiscreminately bucherd. 180, were left dead, those that could, made their Escape, the best way they could. The Tam party, contenplated an attack, on The French of Kaskaskia

[p. 99¹⁴]
and they Selected, the time, the Citizens were at Church, to make the attack, while at Mass they were warnd, it is said by Squaws, of the intended, move. The alarn was given, all prepared White & black, to defend themselves. Those who had guns, went for them. The Negros pickd. any thing, they could, take hold of, hoes axes, spades. The Negers would vie with their Masters in feats of bravery. It Seems a portion of the Indians, had crossd. the Kaskia River, while the people were at Church. Those that had crossd the River, were panic Struck when, they, saw the Inhabitants, ready to recieve them. In their attempt, to recross the River maney were killd. Especially by the Negers. Negers in them days loved their Masters, as they would now, if the abolitionist, would leave them alone. To return to 'Lexi, as I remarkd. above some sixty years ago, the Keekapoos, were in the habit of making periodical raids on the Kaskias. They would come, five or six miles of Town, and lay & watch, Till, they would get their victim

[p. 99¹⁵]
Scalp & go. One fine moring, in the month of may he left with the view, to be gone all day. He proceded North, about six Miles. While lookig out for game he heard as he supposed a Gobler. He immediatly got down, & began with the wing bone, immitate a turkey hen, which he

could do admirably. All at once, as he remarkd. to me, he became Suspecious of that gobbling, which seemd to him unnatural. All this while, he Stood behind a large oak, and assertain if possible the fact, whether it was a Turkey or not, as he could not see, him for the gobling came, behind a large fallen tree. So he put one ear, to the grond. If it was a Turkey the noise, would strke the upper ear, if a human, the noise would strik, the ear next to the Ground. (Wheather, this is so or not I am unable to say.) He soon discoverd. that the gobbler, was a man, and as he justly Supposed, a Keekapoo, so he preposed himself for the horse. His heart for a moment beat quick.

Still Emitating the turkey hen, all at once, the object, of his solicitude, made his appearance, by showing his head, above the fallen tree. He lost no time, in taking aim and sped, his bullit, in the Indian's trotle. I give this as I got it. Som have belivd and others have doubted. He told me that Docter Fisher who livd. within a mile of the plac saw the dead Indian, but never, knew who k...d him. He kept it a Secret, for fear his life would Eendangerd.

[p. 99[16]]
As I have, no date, when, he made his best lick at, Hunting, they must occured betweens 1790 & 1810, for he was in his prime. As I must pass many of his feats, as a Modern Nimrod, I relalate one more of this little, but Extreordinary Man. The facts as related by him was told me by other, as true; and when we come to reflect, how it happend, he Stood, behind a large three, without ever Stering & kill fifty bears. It happen in this Wise, this happen a few mils bellow New Madrid, near the big Swanp. He came across a trail of Migrating bears. He saw that track were fresh, he took, a Stone a Short distance from the trail and in less than half a day, he Shot &

kill, there fifty bear, and remarkd had he been dispod. he could have kill as maney next day, for they were continially going for several days. They Migrated from Kentuckey, to now the State of Missouri. There Swamp back of New Madrid, were always famous bear oil. The French, calld. it <u>L'ancey a la Gresseance</u>. Means, a bend in the River, & Gress oil or grece. This is easily beleivd, when we consider, the migration of the animals.

[p. 99¹⁷]

I must over his hunting feats, and relate a few incidents of his tracking faculties. Several Gentlemen from Kentuckey, by way of Vincennes, had arived at Kaskaskie and lost their Horses. Lexi was Summond, and dispachd. after the Horses. They had swam, the Kaskie River some distance above the ferrey, and struck a bee line towards Vincennes. This Doza soon discoverd. He found where they had crossd, trail a few mils across the River, which was a difficut thing to do as the leaves were falling, frequently, he had to travel several Rods on his knees, in order, to assertain their course Which he did, after following them, several miles. After, assertaining their Course, and about Twenty Miles from Kaskaskie, They Struck, the trail leading to Vincennes. He followd them, two days on said trail. When the tract, was lost, he soon found out when, where they left the trail. Not discourge, he soon found the way they were going. He had to go very slow, for it seems had not eat any thing since they had left. He pursud. them, to a rich bottom of the Little Wabash, where they had remain about a day in feeding, & resting. Said he now it seems

[p. 99¹⁸]

they had made up their mind, to baffle all my Endeavours

to recover them. He spent nearly half a day on his knees to assertain again, the course, they would take which after following about a mile he soon got on a new and Fresh Signe, which greatly pleasd him. Said to me, I knew, I had them. He found them ten miles, from the trail, heading twords Kentuckey. When Warren Brown, them tresorer of the Land office at Kaskaskie, robd. the office of $6000, saying the Roberry was done by two men, who entered his office, while counting the money, and bound his hands behind his back about midnight, he went to house of Register Major Humphey, downd the Major, by bumping his head against his Door. Earley in Moring, Doza and <u>Capt. Tunis</u> were put on the track of the Robers. The plan was pretty well laid, but not to Escape the Vegilance, of Lexi. It seemd. Brown had an accomplice, in this Roberry, as it afterwards turnd out. They had gone about ½ mile, in the commins & returnd. It was very easy to trail them in the Sandy Streets but when they got in the commins, nothing but

[p. 99¹⁹]

short blew-grass, it was very hard, to trail them and had it not been for a light dew they could not have succeeded. Lexi, was up to them. He Could see the impressin of their feet, followd. them on his knees, saw how far they went and when they returnd. This was satisfactey, yet, some had such Confidence in Brown, they could not believe it, and set aside, the Science, of Lexi, as a tracker. But he was right, as Brown, in less than one year Confessd. his guilt, and refunded some of the Money.

I am going to close by, telling one one of the best incident one of the very best but to realise, its intrinsick beauty and animus, one ought to be acquainted, with the different Characters who figgured in it. Doza of mediam size about five seven, Wm Morrisson good size, rather corpulent Speaking broken French, Priest Maxwell, was a tall Irishman, about 6 feet 2 inches. This is the trioo which figgure, but Lexi the most prominant among them. About the time Louisiana, was ceded to the U.S. a Kentuckian, with a Wench & a mulato cheeld about ten years old, Understanding that Priest Maxwell wanted to buy a servant, so he he Struck a bargain, with reverance for $400 thre was no pepper money in them days. The fellow staid about St Genevieve for several days, enjoying himself with the French inhabitants of that place. In his walks on the Bank of the Missisippi he discoverd a canoe at what is now call, the Little Rock Landing, about two miles above the Town of St Genevieve.

[p. 99²⁰]

The fellow had managed to still the women & chield and by means of the canoe or dugout, he cross over to Illinis. As were no roads to guide, them, they had to travel thro,the woods, aiming, to cross, the Kaskaskie River high up, than if possible, strike the trail, from Kaskie to Shawnee Town, and would have done so, had it not been for Lexi, who was the proper man, to frustrate all such undertaking. The momment, it was assertain, they had absconded, The cry, was Doza Doza. Immediatly a courier, was, to Kaskie in order to procure, the assistence of Lexi.

[p. 99²¹]

Mr Wm. Morrisson (The Father of the unfortunate James of yur place by Mr Maxwell, by all means to Secure, the help of Lexi. It was impossible, to overtake them, without him, so Mr. Morrisson, sent for Doza and infirm hm what had happen and his assistance, requird.

Immdiatly he consented to go, with one condition, that was if they overtook them, (who had one day the start) he would not obligate, to take them, as he frequently told me, he rather, face a Red Skin all the time than a Kentuckian, those prelimonaries, ... entered that Doza Should not in any Shape whatever.

From his knowledge, of the county, he knew

[p. 99²²]

pretty well, where to Strike their tracks. Mr Maxwell in the mean while, had cross over to Kaskaskie, and was at Mr Morrisson house Waiting for Doza, who had gone home for his horse, Rifle & tomahock, his constant Companion. Lexi was not formley introduced to his Reverance as such, but simply Mr Maxwell after travelling about six miles, through a rich and aluvial bottom, they assended the Hills what we term, open, meaning wood & Perarie he requested Mr. Morisson & the Stranger as he call the Priest, to remain where they were, as he was anxtius, to find out, where they had assended the Hill, which he did in the course of an hour. They followd. him, to where, he had seen, what he knew to be their tract. Those signes were impervious to their vesinary. They could not see, but left it to Lexi, and abide by his Superior faculties. Freqrently he would Spur his horse, give a little hoop, go on a gallop for fifty yards, them stop. This he done repeatedly. He would, occasionally, show them where they bent the grass. Occasionally they could not

[p. 99²³]

sepress a laugh, which, was not, altogether pleasing, as he thught making fun of him. Altho Lexi, could speek vey good English yet he could comprehend, Morisom and the

Priest, had got in their head, that Lexi was fooling them, that there was no tract to be seen. Mr Maxwell told Morisson, better give up that Doza was deceiving them, that ther was no tract to be seen, it was foolish to follow him any longer. Lexi, supposing Mr Maxwell was making fun of him Monsieur Morisson si il fuist pas son recanage (laughing) je m'en vais l'envoyer au diable, avec la negresse et son batard. Morisson, in bad French, Lexi vous pas parlez com sa — Sa the Ministre. Lexi would answer bak, sa the ministre Englais. This would tickel the Priest, who was full of fun. A little farther Still on the tract, saw by the trampling of the grass, they had Stop, to steping a few feet aside, he where the chield had perform certain functions, indispensable to nature,

[p. 99²⁴]
Monsier Morisson, dite a cel Enfant de Garce, de renei Sentir — tell that son of Whore, to come & smell, it seems he had made Doza mad. The Priest was tickel, to death, to see the earnesness of end honesty of purpose. Marisson, in bad French, this is the Minister this the curé — bak, curé, Englais, meaning a protestant, minister, for whom, he had no venerence. No, no, c'est ca, the curé de St Genevieve, Morisson would reply. At last Mr. Maxwell, in Excellent French, told Lexi, he beg his pardon, for having doubted his word, he was now fully Satisfied. As they went, after travelling a few miles, they come to a deserted cabin, surrounded by high weeds. Lexei jusly suppose, there were in that Cabin. He went alone, on been ... soon return, with the glad Tiding they were there. Now comes the rub. It was perfectly agreed, and stipulated, that Lexi, should have nothing to do with it, for he was

Naturally, afraid, of of Kentuck, as he call them, so the
Priest, and Morisson presented themselves in Front of the
Cabin Door, demanded Surender, then was two parties to
this contract, the Kentuckian, Step out, the Door, with a
long knife. The appearance of such dangerous weapon,
soon put a quietens to the demand. The onley hope was
to enlist, Doza & unless he help them, they never Expected in arresting him. At last by hard persuation and
reward, he agree after maney Excuses. Figure to yourself
a small man sharp eye dress in buck Skins, an old wool
hat with a long knife in his belt, Tomahock & Rifle, all
portaking, of smoke & greese. He Step forword making a
kind of justiculotin, stamping on the ground and saying to
the already frighten men, Godam, Godam Ill Never Shoot
never Shoot, meanig, he would Shoot the appearance of
the man, his simmig determination perfectley quaild. our
man, so he surended to the great releif, to the pursuers,
who return home with their money minus some forty Dollars, and giving the Kentuckian & his negress Carte
Blanche.

Priest Maxwell, was a strict observer of his duty as a
Priest, yet love a joke, as well as Abraham. He use to delight, in telling, how Doza acted, some time in full callop,
on a bending blade of grass, which to him was imper-
cettible. I will close Dear Sir, by adding a transaction,
which occurd in Kaskaskie, about fifty years Ego, and
which Doza use to relate, as he was one of the Witnesses.
This will show you the characters & animus of our Earley
Settlers. Mr Wm Morisson, had sent, a kill, Boat, to
Pittsburg, with Compliment of French Boat Men, under
the charge of my nole John H. Menard. Before they left,

Pittsburg on their return my oncle wrote, to Morisson, they would Short of provisions and to send some, at, the mouth of the Ohio River, now Caro. He sent them, Sour Pickle Pork not fit to eat. At Caro, in consequence of the bad provision, they left, the boat under the care of one man, and footed to Kaskaskia 100 miles. Morrisson re-fud. to pay them. This brought on a Suit by my oncle & the Boat hands. Anticipating, their intentions, he securd. the services of Daniel P. Cook, one of the most eminent Lower of his days. The Boat Men, were compell

[p. 99²⁷]

to take, a mongrel Lawer by the name of Hecock and as it turn out, they could not have made a better Selection. My oncle who, was really, the plamer, knwing that, Morisson had the Low on his side and by far the best lawer, their fist object was to Secure a county Jurey, and work on their feeling & sempaty. They were successfull in this as Eny juror, prone to be. Cook open his case, with plenty of <u>Law Books</u> to help him out. Some Jurors said after the trial was over, had made up their mind, from the argument & the Laws, to give it favour of Morisson. In the mean while Hecock had sent, for a 16 feet pole, with a socket at one End and a nob at the other End. He got up and told the Judge there were two side, to a Story so it was in law suits. Turning round to the Jurey: Here are my clients, look at them. Like you, they are hard working men, like you they Earn their living by the Swet of their Brows. He advance, near a long table, where, the Laws Books were. My friend Mr. Cook, has use these Books to great adventage, as he supposes, may be he has. I dont want them, I have no use for such instruments. Taking the Books in his hands, and dashing them from one End of the Table to the other, Helter Skelter away with them. He than took his coat off, & eying the pole & dresing the Jacket in the wash board, and in immitation, of an Expert Boat put his Shoulder on the knob, pushing with all his might. The Jurey look at him, his ... posture, which he kept, for ten minutes with eyes ready to pop out of their head — he all this while pleading their poverty, and the hardship they Endured. This was sufficient; in five minutes, they returnd with a Virdict, for the plentiff. I have give you a rough sketch of Doza life, all of which I can vouch for Except the Killing of the Indians; it may be. I am sorry you did not come here as I might have done better with your essistence. If you Should deem advisable, any part, make what corrections you may seem proper.

Your P Menard

[p. 100]

Tremont April 9th 1868

L C Draper

D Sir, Your letter of the 10th Septr. 1867 was recd here during my absence & mislaid, never saw it untill was moving. So far as your inquiries goes I can in part, answer them. Once I knew a goodeal more, than I do now.

George R Clark, is from hear say, that his subordinates, spent, a whole winter in Kaskaskie, and as far as my recollection, a mutual good understang Existed betwixt them, & the Inhabitants. The General, made his headquarter at in Michelle Antaya. Clark died in Louisville, he had become very intemporate and died poor. So did his frend Antaya. They meet in Louisville very much reducd in circumstance, Embrace Each other without being able, to utter a word. I hold this from my Father, who knew them both. A Captain Bentley, maried, a great

Aunt of mine, they move to Vincennes; this is all I recollect of them.

[p. 100¹]
I believe, left no children. Layton White Settle in the Neighbourhood, of Keskaskia had children, & they may be som living; of this I am not Certain. Rutherford, Settle in St Clair County. I only kew him by name. Shadrach Bond Ser. died in what is call American Bottom in Monroe County. Kid also died at that place. I knew him. Joseph Anderson, in Randolph Couty he has great many grandchildren in that couty. Biggs Payson died in St Clair couty. John Doyle was my School Master, he died in Kaskie & the grandchildren living. Capt Stacy McDonough, settle, within four Miles of Kaskia. In a moment of desperation, from a long sore leg, he put an End, to life about 45 years Ego by putting a knife, to his neck wich put an end to his Existence. Hughes his brother in Law lived neighbour to him. He died about the same time. I knew Camp & Langford, but dont know what did become of them. As for the Expedition, of Brady & Maillet, I only have a confuse Idea of these.

Genl. Whiteside, died some Twenty years

[p. 100²]
Ego in Monroe Conty he has left som decendants in that County. As for Pointe Sable the Mulotoe, I knew his history, once but have really forgeoten. I would refer you, to J G Toulard of Galina, or Judge Wilson Prim of St Louis, they could tell you more about him.

As for the Indian cheefs Black Bird & Ja-Ke-Wani I knw nothing of them. I knew white bird, & Senachwani of the Poutowatami tribe. I knew Pacan, a Piankesha a branch of the Miami, if the Sanees. He died on White

River in Missouri & if alive, he would be about 90 perhaps more. As for Gov Leyba Judge Prim will tell you all about him. This is all the information, my poor memory Will Sugest. If you Should publish a Book of the earley Settlement of this Western country I Should like to have a coppy. I wish I could give you more information. 40 years I was quite conversant with the Expedition G R Clerk

Respectfully yours
P Menard

[p. 100³]

If the Cheif <u>Packen</u> is the one I have before me he had a complete controul over his band or tribe, consisting of about two fifty all told. They obeyd. him, Even, to the greatest absordity. They look on him, as an intermediate betwixt the great Spirit, & them. The French call him <u>La hache</u> (the ax).

[p. 101]

Tremont, Dec 3d 1870
L C Draper

My dear Sir. I have just recd yours of the 26 Uto. which gave me pleasure and I cordially thank you for the two pamflets sent to my address. It is so long since, I heard from you I did suppose you had gone to that abode where the Just meets. As for myself I did not suppose the last time I commencated I would be at this time a Tenant of this house. My abode is yet here. I am I am full of years. My Wife & myself right away we read ... Honle Orton address. My wife fully agrees with him about the age of this world. Myselfe altho I admier the address yet it is all Speculation. Every thing is grand & misterious & when I look at that great Historian Moses, & the prophets

I & believe in their computation as the old saying is right or wrong. I would be glad to give you desird information about Col John Thomas.

[p. 101¹]
    Since I recd yours I Spent a couple of hours in looking over Govr John Reynolds early Settlement of Illins. I could not find the name of John Thomas. There is however, a famly of Thomas in St Cliar County & near Bellville one Col. Thomas was in Black Hawk war, & it is my impression, this Col Thomas was born in Kol Couty. At any rate the name is very famlier as far back as I can recolect. He may be a son of the Subject of your serch. If you wish I will make the inqiry. Have you got the History of Ms by Reynolds it is very intersting Especialy to me, who knew most of the Leading Men. If you have not got it I will send to you with the proviso you will send it back as the Book dont belong to me. Judge Breese has compild a new history of this State but does not know whether he will publish it. If he does I make no doubt it will Excell all others in Stile & deep research.
    Belive deer Sir my best wishes for your health & properity
                                    P Menard

[p. 102]
Letters from Benjamin Scott
                    O'Fallon, Illinois, Jan 14, 1863
Mr. Draper:
    You will please Excuse me for not writing Sooner. My mother from home I expected to get the most of my information was Sick. She is in her 87th year, blind, in this spell of Sickness has lost her hearing. She is on the mend now but her mind is pretty near gone. She was here

when the widow <u>Moredock</u> came to this country. Her husband <u>Daniel Moredock</u> was killed in Kentucky by the Indians; then the widow came to this country with two Children. One child died at Vincennes, Indiana. She brought John & Barney with her. She was not here long till She maried a man by the name of

[p. 102¹]
Ferrell. In Some six or eight months Ferrell was killed by the Indians. Mother cannot say how long till She maried Michael Huff. Huff was killed by the Indians; then She maried McFall her fourth & last husband. She then went to Kentuckey on a visit to See her father I cannot Say in what part of Kentucky, Leaving her two Sons here. She never had any children by her three last husbands three children are all She ever had. They were Moredocks. On her returne home Some place about the mouth of the Ohio She was killed by the Indians. The two Sons, John & Barney were here. Barney after he got to be a young man, went to Kentuckey & died there. John lived & married in this country had Some Six or Seven children.

[p. 102²]
His children all died but one before he did. She has died Since. The Moredock family has become extnct there none none of the family living. John Moredock was one of the most portley men I ever saw, about Six feet high Square maid & well proportioned weighing about 200 pounds active for a man of his size would walk all day in the woods hunting. He was a great hunter for all kinds of game. I have heared him say he neve let the chance Slip for killing a Indian when hunting. He raised a compny & went to an island in the Mississippi river & killed Six or eight Indians at one time. He Said he never would make

peace

[p. 102³]
with the Indians as long as he lived. I doe not think he ever did. Colonel Moredock bcame Rich in land & property, but cared nothing for it; he Spent it as fast as it came. It came by his Stepfather, they having no heirs. If any trouble got up by Indians Moredock was one of the first to go all ways comanding the company. He was in the war of 1812. All the time he was a great gambler in any way wit a gun which he all ways carried & kept in the best of order. One of the most benevolent men I ever saw. He has given thousands of dollars to away. I think he neve paid any attention to his family ... of gambleing at cards or Samething else.

[p. 102⁴]
    All about his father is that he was killed in Kentukey by Indians. John became vary disepated & when Drinking quarrelsom. He Served in the legislature one or two Sessions. Was Major in the war of -1812- on Edwards Campaign.
    About Colonel Moredock's Fatther I cannot Say any thing more: I take all of this from Mother's account — onley what I have said about the collonel.
                    Yours with Rspect
                    Benjamin Scott

    Memo. by L.C.D. There was a John Moredock killed on Bowmans Campaign, May, '79, who had a brother Edward: See Note Book, small size, No. 7, 1845.

[p. 102⁵]
    NB. if there is any more that I can write you Send

me word & I will & writee Sooner

B Scott

[p. 103]

O'Fallon Jan. 29, 1863

Mr Draper, Dear Sir:

I Receved yours of the 22d and hasten to answer it Sooner than the other letter I received from you. My mother is here but her mind and hearing are pretty Mucth gone; it is very hard to make her understand any thing. I will give you the best information I can get. Mother has no relationship with with the Moredock family whatever: my wife was a niece of Moredock's wife. We are no other way related. Mother was born in Westmoreland County pennsylvania in the year 1776 came to this county the 1786 in the spring.

[p. 103¹]

After they came to this country in the fall they went into the fort called <u>Piggot's Fort</u> on the edge of the bottom, now Monroe county; her madin name was Kinkead her fathers name was <u>James Kinkead</u>, an Irishman by birth. Mother thinks that <u>Daniel</u> was the given name of old man <u>Moredock</u> & thinks he was in Clarks armey; he was killed in a battle in Kentuckey but is not certain. She can't Say how old the Colonel was when his father was killed; She thinks <u>10</u> or 12 years old, not older.

Mother thinks She was about <u>12</u> or 14 years old when widow came to the country. They was in the fort at at the time widow Moredock came to the country.

Moredock killed the Indans about the year 1801 or 2. We cannot Say what the name of the island was. It goes by the name of Beard's Island now, about 18 or 20 milse below St. Louiss.

Mother remembers Layton White & Logston & Fallenash, but cannot give any particulars about those men.

Colonel Moredock Died in monroe county & was buried there on the farme of old Judge Bond: not governor Bond; there is no Stone at his grave I do not think. There was not 8 or 10 years ago. That is about 30 miles from my place altho I was born & raised there, but left there 33 years ago.

If you wish any more Information I will give you all I can. You will please write a little plainer as I am not much of a Scholar.

That you have found out before this time.

Yours with much Respect

Benjn Scott

L C Draper

Land claim of Rachael Murdock

In 1806: "The heirs of Rachael Murdock claim 400 acres, on the waters of the River Du Chis, in right of improvement.

Jonathan Conger, in his deposition filed & registered, states that he, deponent, cut logs, deadened trees, laid the foundation of a cabin, and made several brush heaps for Rachel Murdock, on the land now claimed, and could do more, on account of the Indians. When brought before the commissioners to be examined, viva voce, he stated that Rachel Murdock employed him to clear about one acre of the land claimed; that he planted it in corn and

fruit trees; that she lived about four years in the [Vencennes] country, when she went to the Illinois, where she was killed by the Indians." Claim disallowed on account of contradiction of the deponent in his description.
Am. State Papers Public Lands i, 275.

In 1813. Land Claims.

"Rachael Moredock — claimed by her heirs: Proof & remarks: That she was head of a family in the Illinois before 1788, and until she was killed, after 1788, by the Indians." Claim for 400 acres as head of a family, in Kaskaskia district, was allowed.

In 1813. "Michael Huff, by his heirs, allowed 400 acres. That he was head of a family from 1787 until he was killed by the Indians in 1794. This man had a militia right. See No. 1418.
Am. State Papers, Public Lands, ii, 614.

[p. 105]
Pioneer Sketch. Joseph Ogle, Sr.
One of the Patriarchs of Illinois

"We rustled through the trees like wind,
Left shrubs, and trees, and foes behind;
By night I heard them on the track,
With their long gallop which can tire,
The hounds deep hate and hunter's fire."
Byron's "Mazeppa."

The student of our country's history cannot but but be deeply impressed with that portion immediately after the settlement of the infant colonies, and prior to the Revolution. King Philip's, and the murderous French and Indian wars, were the most conspicuous events, at that early day. During the latter, Pennsylvania, New York and Virginia, sent to the field, in connection with the Eastern States, some of their gallant sons, who soon after won a name in fighting for human rights, that shall be as enduring as time itself.

At that early day, Fort Du Quesne, near the junction of the Alleghany and Monongahela rivers, afforded a kind of nucleous, around and from which the French and Indians made their sallies upon the adjacent settlements. To dislodge them from this point was the great effort of the Americans and English. It was upon such a mission that Braddock started with his fine army, which was finally saved and extricated from total annihilation by one who seemed endowed with ubiquity. But this is matter of history.

In the midst of such scenes, the character of Joseph Ogle was formed. Too young to take the field against the French and Indians, yet he was enabled to do some important service about his home, during the absence of his sire in the field. At a later period he volunteered, when barely able to wield the unerring rifle. But it is not my purpose to enter into a biographical sketch of his life. I only purpose relating a single incident in his career, which he used to term his "narrow escape," leaving to the historian of our state (Rev. J. M. Peck) the pleasant task of furnishing the public with the general outline of his life.

Among our first settlers, he was contemporary with the Whitesides, Stouts and John Murdock. Soon after the termination of the Revolutionary war, he left his native home in Pennsylvania, and accompanied by his young family started for Illinoise, the then Far West.

He soon reached Pittsburgh, formerly Fort Du Quesne. The old fort had long been destroyed, and at that particular period the inhabitants made use of a few strong, substantial, block houses, as a means of defence against their savage neighbors, who made occasional irruptions into the settlements.

Ogle tarried at this place for some time, for the purpose of collecting provisions for his long journey, and hear, if possible, from below. He had hopes, too, of obtaining company, as the summer months were well advanced, on his perilous journey, in which he partially succeeded.

During his sojourn in Pittsburgh, a considerable number of horses and cattle were suddenly missing, and from the "sign," so easily detected by the early backwoodsmen, it was evident that hostile Indians were prowling about, which readily accounted for the loss of the stock.

The settlement becoming alarmed, hastily gathered into the block houses. Upon consultation, it was resolved to send out a few of the bravest men for the purpose of hunting after the lost cattle, and to ascertain certainly if the savages were near at hand. Joseph Ogle who readily volunteered, was deputed to take the most hazardous route. Waiting for the sun to get well up, and dry off the heavy dew of the night previous; to prevent their trail being easily followed, the party sallied forth upon their errand. Ogle had advanced about a mile from the fort, and had just passed a wild region of scrub oak, thorn, shumac, and alders, a fine hiding place, when he became aware of the immediate presence of Indians. A shot glancing forward under his left arm, and tearing away a small strip of his leather hunting frock, but too plainly told him that his foes had gained his rear, and were between him and his friends. His eagle eye took in the danger with which he was surrounded, at a glance. Poising his rifle in his hands, as the puff of smoke gently waved away from whence the shot had been fired, he brought it to a level, and the next moment its clear report rang through the distant hills, as an Indian sprang up from behind a bush, where he had lain concealed, and, with a yell, bounded but once forward, and was dead!

There was no time for re-loading. — Ogle did not even wait to see the effect of his shot — he knew full well what it would be when he fired — but bounded away at the top of his speed for a large cornfield lying about three-quarters of a mile distant. The main body of Indians soon broke cover, and came yelling on his rear like a pack of demons.

Full well he knew his fate was sealed if once in their clutches. Giving a thought to his then helpless family, entirely dependant on him for support, and knowing they would be under the most painful apprehensions as to his safety, did he not return by nightfall, he sped on!

The cornfield, with its tall waving grain was just before him. Once in it, with his trusty rifle, and he would feel comparatively safe, as he was sure none of his pursuers would venture singly into the field to hunt him out. But how to cross the fence (a stake-and-rider fence nine rails high) and retain his gun at the same time, was the all absorbing question to his mind. To clamber over would give his foes time to shoot, as they were barely beyond long rifle range. Cross the fence he must, if he wished to save his scalp, and if he wished to retain an equal chance for his life, his gun must go with him.

Straining his nerves to their utmost tension, when about fifty yards from the fence, and measuring a pannel with his eye, he approached it in a short quick running step, striking about four rails high

[p. 106]
with one of his feet, and catching at the rider (top-rail) with his left hand, he vaulted over, gun in hand, so easily, that he afterwards said it

astonished himself. — Casting a furtive glance behind as his feet struck the ground on the opposite side, he saw his foes standing in mute amazement. A simultaneous "Wagh!" from the entire party was the only exclamation of wonderment from them.

Of course he did not stop to explain the philosophy of jumping a nine rail fence, with a gun in his hand — it was new even to him — but darted off into the corn, at an angle in the direction of the fort, to mislead his pursuers. He saw them scattering, before he was out of sight, for the purpose of surrounding the field. The ground within the field (thanks to the same Indians for preventing its culture) was covered with a thick matting of crabgrass upon which the foot of one man would scarcely leave an impression.

Retaining a stooping posture, a tall man could keep perfectly concealed in the field to which Ogle had escaped. So soon as he was far enough within the corn to be beyond the range of a rifle, he re-loaded, and then commenced a series of gyratory evolutions for the purpose of throwing his pursuers off his trail, in the event of their following him into the field.

He soon satisfied himself that they had not entered the field, and feeling assured that they were still watching for him, he struck out in a direction for the fort, and soon had the good fortune to strike a point on the edge of the field, where an enormous tree had been blown down.

The rank weeds had grown to an unusial height around the trunk and roots of the fallen monarch of the forest. Without disturbing the almost "audible stillness," Ogle quietly slid into a small open space at the root of the tree, where he could barely see beyond the fence, which was not a rod off, so thick were the weeds by which he was surrounded.

Quietly seating himself with his rifle across his knee, he drew forth from a side pocket a single morsel of jerked venison and a tickler of pure water, from which he drew a refreshing draught.

Hours rolled by — twelve o'clock had passed, and no sound of lurking foe — and Ogle began to hope all danger was past, when suddenly he heard the cat like tread of approaching footsteps! Nearer and nearer their stealthy tread came until he was enabled to distinguish the approach of two.

But a few steps more, and they stopped nearly opposite to where he lay. Quick as lightning his thumb was on the cock and forefinger on the trigger; the next moment revealed the features of two of his pursuers. A glance at their leaden gaze told him, more readily than words, that they were not aware of his proximity.

Leaning their guns against the fence, they quietly clambered up, and seated themselves on the top rail, in doing which they threw down one from the adjoining pannel, which fell within a yard of where Ogle lay, but their stolid features were not even turned in that direction by the occurrence.

One drew forth a pipe, which he soon filled, lighted, and commenced smoking, passing it to his companion, at the same time invoking their "medicine" to assist in exterminating the whites. Their conversation, made up of a few short guttural sounds, mingled with signs, plainly indicated to Ogle that he was the burden of their them.

Meanwhile the sun was wheeling its course rapidly down in the West. The shadows of the adjacent trees began to be lengthened out, the millions of insects composing a part of the "orchestra of nature," commenced tuning their pipes for the evening serenade, and all nature indicated the near approach of night. Still the savages continued to occupy the same position. At last there came a call, as familiar to there enemy as themselves, and in obedience they quietly glided from the fence, picked up their guns, and silently struck out for the forest.

As the evening wore on, and darkness covered the earth, Ogle left his concealment, and started for the fort. His limbs were quite rigid from retaining one posture so long, and his fingers seemed like sticks.

He reached the fort in safety, just as his friends were starting out in force to search for him.

A few days after his race he started for Illinois, which he reached in safety, and settled in Ridge Praire, where he lived to a good old age, and died lamented by numerous relatives and friends. Around his memory twined many pleasing recollections. His remains now rest in the burying-ground of Shiloh valley, near the flourishing town of Bellville.

Other names in the history of our country may be inscribed higher upon the scroll of fame, but a truer heart never beat in human breast than that of Josepth Ogle. — *Spirit of the Times.*

"Great West" — Cincinnati, Feb. 9, 1850.

[p. 107]
Letters from James Lemen
Collinsville Madison Co. Illinois
January 18th 1863

My Dear Brother:

Tottering under the weight of 75 years I have seated myself for the purpose of complying with your request. At the time your first letter came to hand such was my affliction that I was unable to write. I hope therefore you will not attribute my silence to any want of respect, but to my advanced age and feeble health.

Captain Joseph Ogle, (who was my Grandfather on my mother's side) was a native of Virginia, born 1738. He resided at Wheeling during the Revolutionary War and held a Captain's commission [which commission is now in my possession] signed by Patrick Henry, then Governor of Viriginia, June 2nd 1777. In 1785 he removed to Illinois and located in St Clair County, where he remained until his death in 1821. His family was large consisting of three sons & six daughters all of whom lived to become heads of families but have since passed away. We should have said in its proper place, that under his Commission from Gov. Henry, Capt. Ogle Commanded the fort at Wheeling. His oldest son Benjamin, when but a youth was severely wounded by the Indians and carried the ball with him to his grave; but upon becoming grown he avenged himself on his foes by killing & scalping one of the same tribe by whom he had been wounded. In this skermish were Capt. Joseph

[p. 107¹]
Ogle, my father, and Benjamin Ogle with four others, making in all seven whites, against nine Indians: five indians were killed, two wounded & two escaped; while the whites sustained no loss. Shortly after this bloody battle Benjamin Ogle made a profession of religion, and became a minister of the gospel in the Baptist denomination, & devoted the last forty years of his life to the labors of the Gospel Ministry. He departed this life in February

1847 in the 77 year of his age.

William Biggs was a native of Virginia and was brother-in-law of Capt. Jos. Ogle, the latter having married the sister of the former. I cannot state the exact period of his birth. I am inclined to think however that he was born in 1754. He was a soldier in the distinguished army with which Gen. G. R. Clark performed his western expedition; & aided in the capture of St. Post Vincent, Kaskaskia, & Cahokia. After returning to Virginia & receiving an honorable discharge from service, he went to Wheeling there married, & shortly after returned to Illinois. His first daughter (first child) being born on the Mississippi on his journey to Illinois, he gave her the name of Mississippi. He settled in St. Clair County where he remained the balance of his life. In 1788 he was taken prisoner by the Indians & carried to the Kickapoo town on the Wabash, whence he was finally liberated by means of the French traders. He was a member of the Territorial Legislature for some six or seven years, & for many years Judge of the County Court. Not long before his death he wrote & published an account of his capture & sufferings among the Indians; & in person presented it to Congress, upon which he

[p. 107²]

received a donation of several hundred acres of land. He had seven children, two sons & five daughters; whether any of them are now living I do not know. I cannot give you the precise periods of either the birth or death of Judge Biggs. I am pretty confident he was born in 1754 & died 1830.

James Lemen Senior (who was my father) was born in Berkeley County Virginia 1760. He served two years in the Revolutionary war under General Washington. After the close of the war he visited a brother in law who was residing at Wheeling, when he became acquainted with Capt. Joseph Ogle & family & married his oldest daughter. In 1786 he followed his father in law Capt. Ogle to Illinois & settld in St. Clair County, where he spent the remainder of his life. He was I believe the first acting Justice of the Peace under the American laws in Illinois. After serving for some time as Justice of the peace, he was appointed Judge of the Court of Common Pleas, which office he held for a number of years. At length he entered the Gospel Ministry, & devoted the balance of his days almost exclusivly to preaching the Gospel, and died on the 8th day of January 1823 in the 63rd year of his age. He however lived to see his whole family of children, (eight in number, six sons & two daughters) all become heads of families, & members of churches in the Baptist denomination; also to see four of his sons (Joseph, Josiah, Moses & myself all in early life) inducted into the Gospel Ministry, with whom he was permitted to mingle his labors for several years. Robert (our oldest brother) Joseph, William, Moses & sister

[p. 107³]
Nancy Tolin are now with those beyond Jordan While Josiah, Sister Catharine Harlow & myself still linger this side the Cold stream.

With regard to Joseph Lemen the Indian fighter mentioned in your letter I have no knowledge. My brother Joseph was by no means an Indian fighter, but a pious Minister of the Gospel for the space of fifty years. He however has a son by the name of Joseph, who was a captain in the Mexican War, & was with Gen. Taylor in many of his hard-fought battles, & is now commanding a

Company in our present unhappy war against the Southern rebels.

Fraternally Yours, James Lemen

P. S. Upon a more mature reflection I am inclined to think that the name of Lemen, through mistake, has been substituted for Ogle, and that Joseph Ogle instead of Joseph Lemen was the noted Indian fighter refered to in your letter. Capt. Joseph Ogle in both Virginia & Ills. was everywhere spoken of by all who knew him as "the great Indian warrior." He distinguished himself at the siege of Fort Henry, & in many skermishes with the Indians in Western Virginia & in Illinois. He was the principal leader in the early excursions against the savages, & was invariably consulted (in matters of war) by the American forts of our country.

At length he became truly pious, & for many years exhibited a consistent christian character and died in the possession of a firm hope of a blessed immortality.

Truly Yours J. L.

[p. 108]

Collinsville Ills. February 12th 1863

Brother Lyman C. Draper:

Having discovered by the reading of your Circular [a copy of which you had the kindness to send me] the vast amount of labor which you have expended in the procurement of material for Western History I would fain assist you all I could, but my advanced age & daily infirmities disqualify me for such labor.

The battle about which you seem to have been puzzled, was fought in Illinois in 1791 some five or six miles Northeast of Waterloo, the present seat of justice of Monroe County. The Indians had stolen several horses, & fired on a certain John Dempsey, who having made his escape, carried the tidings to his friends who siezed their guns, mounted their horses, took the trail of the Indians, overtook them in scattering timber, a battle ensued, which terminated according to my former account. The stolen horses were recovered.

Capt. Joseph Ogle, Benjamin Ogle, James Lemen Sr. Nathaniel Hull, Josiah Ryan, John Porter & Daniel Raper were the names of the seven whites. Conflicting accounts have been given relative to the number of each of the war parties; but my information is from Grandfather Ogle, Benjamin Ogle & my father, who were in the battle.

Grandfather Ogle has no children living. His son Benjamin spent the most of his time for the last five or six years of his life in Iowa, where he had two daughters living. This circumstance doubtless gave rise to your impression, that Grandfather has a son living in Iowa, who is a minister of the Gospel. None of Grandfather Ogle's sons were preachers but Uncle Benjamin, & he died in 1847. [Eighteen & Forty Seven] Five of his children are yet living. Their names are as follows, according to their births: Polly, Nancy, Catharine, Prudence & Jacob. Polly married a man by the name of Solomon Perkins, Nancy a man by the name of Daniel Chance, Catharine a man by name of Reuben Chance, [Daniel's brother],

[p. 108¹]
Prudence a man by name of John Williams. Solomon Perkins, Daniel Chance & wives are living in Iowa. Cannot say what Counties as both have recently changed their places of residence but still remain in Iowa. John Williams & wife are living in Indiana, cannot say what County. Reuben Chance & wife reside Marion County Ills. Jacob Ogle & family are living in St. Clair County Illinois.

Judge Biggs has a granddaughter living in St. Paul Minnesota: her husband's name is Martin Stites. Doubtless he can give you all desirable information relative to the children of their grandfather.

The father of Col. John Murdock was killed by the Indians in Kentucky. The particulars of time & place I cannot specify. In 1788 or 89 the widow of Murdock with her two sons John & Barnabas came to Illinois & located in St. Clair County, where she married a Michael Huff, who in 1794 was killed by the Indians near Kaskaskia. His widow again married a ... by the name of McFall, who shortly after their marriage was also killed by the Indians. After the death of her third husband, the widow McFall set out upon a visit to Kentucky to see her former friends, & was herself killed by the Indians not far from Pos... Vincennes. Thus the father & Mother & two step fathers of Col. John Murdock's were all killed by the Indians. Col. Murdock and Benjamin Ogle were brothers-in-law, having married sisters. The Colonel was a portly fine looking man, & quite popular. He   .lonel of Militia; & for some four or five years a member of the Territorial Legislature. His hostility to the Indians knew no bounds in consequence of they having massacred so many of his near relatives. He was reckless & brave & constantly sought opportunities to wreak his vengeance upon ...

[p. 108²]
as evinced by his attack upon those encamped on an island near St. Louis, of which you made mention. The name of the island, the particulars of the skermish, & also the date have all escaped my memory.

Col. Murdock died in Illinois. I cannot give the exact periods of either his birth or death. He was about the age of Benjamin Ogle; born I am inclined to think in the same year, & there was but a short space between their deaths.

Of the military service of <u>Layton White</u> I know nothing more, than that he was a soldier under Gen. George R. Clark. He was an honest industrious man had no family, never married, lived to an advanced stage of life & died in Madison County Illinois some forty years since.

With the <u>certain dates</u> of many facts mentioned in my letter I cannot furnish you. I have no knowledge of any persons or families the name of Lemen who settled in Illinois some forty & fifty years ago.

While my father was in the Revolutionary service, he was in several severe skermishes, but in no very noted battles. He was quite young when he entered the service. Josiah Lemen my only living brother, is residing in Duquoin Perry Co. Illinois 60 miles south of my residence. Sister Catharine Harlow is living in Monroe County, 40 miles west of me.

Rev. J. M. Peck in his appendix to the "Annals of the West" has given a brief sketch of nearly all the skermishes which took place between the whites & Indians in the early settling of Illinois, together with the names of individuals & families who were killed or taken prisoner by the Indians.

[p. 109]
Which work doubtless you have among the many volumes of your Library.

Fraternally yours
James Lemen Sr.

Obituary of James Lemen Sr.

Rev. James Lemen, last surviving member of the Convention which framed the first Constitution of Illinois, in 1818, died at the residence of his son, near Belleville, the 8th inst.

Chicago Daily Tribune, Feb. 15th 1870

Memo

I called on the preceding Rev. Jas. Leman, in the summer of 1868, but his memory had all faded out, so he could give no information whatever. He seemed kind, was tall, spare, bony, over Six feet high.

L. C. D.

THE STANDARD
Chicago, Thursday, Feb. 24, 1870.
A Patriarch Fallen.

Rev. James Lemen, so well known in Illinois and the West, died at his residence in New Design, St. Clair county, Feb. 8. Thus has been severed another link binding the present to the past. The Lemen family has been in the past and still is a power in Southern Illinois. A record of the Leman family would occupy an important chapter in the history of Illinois, including physical development, morals, religion and politics. A friend has furnished us a brief sketch of the life and labors and last days of the venerable Rev. James Lemen, one of nature's noblemen.

Elder James Lemen was the third son of Rev. James and Catharine Lemen, who emigrated from Virginia to Illinois in 1786. They were the parents of six sons and two daughters, all of whom attached themselves to the Baptist church, and lived to a good old age, each leaving a large family. Four of the sons were active ordained ministers of the Gospel.

Elder James Lemen was born in Illinois, Oct. 8, 1787. He was the second white child, born of American parents, in the State — Enoch Moore being the first. Elder Lemen made a profession of religion about the age of twenty, and immediately commenced preaching, but he did not attach himself to the church till he had fully made up his mind what course to pursue. He then united with the only Baptist church at that time in the State. He was ordained by this church to the work of the Gospel ministry. In 1800 he, in connection with Elder John Baugh, constituted what was then called the Cantine Creek, now Bethel church. Elder Lemen remained a member of this church to the time of his death — over sixty years. For the most of this time he was an active, efficient minister of the Gospel, traveling far and wide, organizing and building up churches, and laboring with marked success in the work of his Master, in Illinois, Missouri, and other Western States. Elder Lemen's father was the first person baptized by immersion in Illinois. The subject of this sketch assisted at his own father's ordination. He preached his father's funeral sermon. His brother Joseph preached that of their mother. Elder Lemen served his native State some sixteen years in the halls of legislation, both as a Representative and a Senator. He was also offered the election to the United States Senate; but, having come to the determination to abandon politics in order that he might devote all his time and talents to the Gospel ministry, he declined the distinguished honor of a seat in the Senate of the United States. He was the last surviving member of the Convention that formed the old State Constitution. For the last few years his health has been such that he has been confined almost entirely to his rooms at home. In the twenty-sixth year of his age, Dec. 8, 1813, he was married to Polly Pulliam. They were the parents of eleven children — six of whom, together with the bereaved mother and widow, are left to lament the loss of their dearest earthly friend. On Tuesday evening, February 8, about 5 o'clock, the labors, and prayers, and suffering of Elder James Lemen were ended.

"How well he fell asleep!
Like some proud river, winding towards the sea,
Calmly and grandly, silently and deep,
Life joined eternity."

"In the great harvest field of Zion he lived and labored long and faithfully, gathering into the fold of Christ a rich harvest of souls. While on the watch-tower of Zion, he fell with his armor on, shouting 'Victory,' as he mounted his chariot and went up to heaven."

His companion being unable to go to Bethel church, brief services were held at his late residence — W. S. Post officiating. His remains were then taken to the church where an immense concourse of his relatives and friends were assembled with moistened eyes and sad hearts to pay the last tribute of respect and affection to the dear departed. The sermon was preached by W. S. Post, Elders Cochran, Roach and Hill assisting in the services. His own son, Sylvester, made some expressive and touching remarks. The singing by the choir was appropriate and beautiful.   W. B. P.

[p. 110]
Letter from Sidney Breese
Carlyle Ill. March 4. / 63

Dear Sir

I had the pleasure to receive a few days since your letter of the 24th. ulto. And in answer have to say, I can afford you no information on the topics you suggest. In Reynolds' History of Illinois you will find a notice of Col. Moredock whom I knew well, but have preserved no facts about him. So with Alexis Doza; I knew him as one of the most sagacious hunters of the land, a remarkable man in his way, and one well known to P. Menard Esq. of Tremont. Of Logston I don't now remember even to have heard. I have Vols. 1 & 2 of Halls Ill. Magazine, but with

[p. 110¹]
every desire to accomodate you, am unwilling they should go out of my library.

I wish you much success in the prosecution of your labors redounding as they will I trust, greatly to your pecuniary and literary benefit.

With great respect
Yr. obt. Se...
Sidney Breese

L. C. Draper Esq.
Cor. Secy. Wisconsin
Historical Society

[p. 111]
Letter from John T. Lusk
Edwardsville Feb 21st 1854

Sir

Yours of August 12th came duly to hand at which

time I was busily engaged in Starting a Saw mill. Your letter was then laid down as I supposed for a few days. I soon had to take a trip south to Mississippi and Arkansas and until recently your letter entirely forgotten but perhaps better late than never. I will now begin to answer some of your enquiries begining with your last first.

I was born in November 1784 in Spartenburg (then County now) District South Carolina. My father emigrated to the western country in the fall of 1798 and in March 99 settled on the bank of the Ohio river fifteen Miles above the mouth of Cumberland at the place that was afterwards called Lusk's ferry where I remained until after the death of my father who died September 1803. In March 1805 I left there and pitched my tent here in this vicinity.

General Lacy lived in the county adjoining that in which I was born my father and him being old acquaintances perhaps in the Revolution about the year 1800 or 1801 I am not certain which. Lacy came to the western country and settled about ten miles from my fathers and lived there for several years at last was drowned in the back water from the Ohio River in a Small creek called deer creek about one mile from his home. That was after I came here. I cannot now tell you where any of his family now lives. He was not conspicuous. He was nothing more than a Bregadier General in the South

[p. 111¹]
Carolina Militia after the Revolution.

Next John Duff. John Michael Duff, with one Fleahart and one William Goin with some others crossed the Ohio River and commenced making salt at what has since been called the Ohio Saline and were broken up by the General Government I think about the year 1798. Fleahart was not at the works at the time and therefore was not taken with the rest. They were taken by Captain Pastures who commanded the Garrison at old Fort Masac and taken to that place to send them down the River for further trial. They were then hobbled two and two with chains and put on board a keel boat under the command of Lieutenant Wilson and started down the river to some other post far below. Goin when hobbled took the precaution to be hobbled on the top of his leather leggin and when dark came on he went to work drew up his leggin under his hobble drew of his sock and then his hobble came easily of both him and his companion they were now both footloose. Lieut. Wilson who had chai of the boat told the soldiers to lie down and take a nap of sleep that he would take the first tour at the helm.. Goin being pretty arch had noticed them load his Rifle and lay her down in the boat before night and having laid some Muskets over board and taken the flints out of others so that they were useless, getting Just out of Sight of the mouth of the Ohio river, observed that he believed they were now out of sight of the point when Wilson turned his head to look Goin seizing the opportunity and his own Rifle Sprang to Wilson with his Rifle cocked and demanded of Wilson his Pistols which he had swung on his belt. Wilson at first denied having any but Goin ordered him to hand them over but foremost without any noise or he would send the

[p. 111²]

load through him, which he then thought best to do. Goin then ordered him to arouse the soldiers and make them row the boat to shore which was done, and they all set on shore. Goin then told them where they might find some of their Muskets. The rumor of the case at that day was that the hobbles were cut off of Duffs leg with an axe and his leg much bruised in the opperation. I became acquainted with Goin after I came here. Duff after being boxed about a while got into a cabbin about the mouth of a small Stream that empties into the Ohio called treadwater and about the last of March or perhaps in April 1799 four Indians supposed at that day to have been sent by one Cribbs who lived at fort Masac went to Duffs and after Staying some two or more days all that time appearing friendly when about to leave two went to shake hands with him, at once and at the same Instant stabbed and killed him put into their canoe and left. I have always thought since the occurance that I saw the Indians as they went up the river a few days before they killed him. As to his being one of the Soldiers of General Clark I cannot tell. I met with Fleahart on the Ohio River and have seen his wife. I think however that he went into Kentucky and persuaded a girl off crossed the Ohio and at a cabbin near the lick her brother who followed found them and shot him. Colonel Hugh Magary did live for some time at or near Hopkinsville Kentucky; was some what wild and I think more of the Busting Bragadocia than real merit in his character. His character I have more from those more acquainted with him than I was myself.

Mason and his band of Robbers I think was between Nashville and Natchez from about 1798 or 1799, until about 1802 or say about three years more or less when after making some considerable draws from those whom they had Murdered and wishing to Move their quarters Mason took with him a <u>choice</u> companion whose name was May and took all the booty in a canoe or other small boat and went down the river to some given point where the others who took their horses was to meet them. Mason and May reached the point of destination first. Mason anxious to know how much they had taken since they had last counted took up a first rate Rifle handed it to May who was standing or sitting in the canoe to stand as sentinel until he would count the money. May thinking this a good time to make a haul cocked the rifle, applied it to his face, thinking if Mason should see him he would say he was only looking to see how neatly he could kill him, but Mason not raising his head May fired the finishing shot for Mason. May then struck for New Orleans with the head of Mason to get the Government reward for the killing. They there let him slope with his life as the only reward he got for killing Mason. That was the end of Mason and his gang according to the history of the day.

Next the Harpes. Stegall made an appointment with a man by the name of Love to come to his house on a certain day to receive a sum of Money he owed him. Love came Stegall not at home he kept waiting until late he not coming home Love concluded to stay all night at an early hour Love went up stairs to bed shortly afterwards the Harpes came (whether by arrangement with Stegall or otherwise not known but some suspicion) and also wished to stay all night. Mrs. Stegall told them to go up stairs to bed. They went up found Love in bed. They Murdered him came down stairs commenced a quarrel with Mrs. Stegall for putting them in a room with a crazy man and also murdered her. Set the house on fire and left the premises in the Morning about Eight Oclock they met a man in the woods by the name of Smith who was horse hunting while they were walking round to get Smith between them that the one at his back might Shoot him which Smith observed and kept walking round so as to keep them both before him. The company who had raised and got on the trail and chase of the Harpes came in Sight. They then broke and left Smith standing. They came rushing on one Leeper in front who saw Smith called out dont Shoot him I know him but Squire Magby a little further back not riding so good a horse seeing Smith Standing rode out of the line Jumped from his horse and Shot Smith through the thigh or hip I am not now certain which (but I think through the hip) fracturing the bone and left him there to get home the best way he could. This I had from Smith himself with whom I afterwards was well acquainted. The company followed on in chase. Leeper at length got near enough to shoot Harpe and bring him to the ground brave men plenty then but the bravest of the brave was Stegall the husband of the woman the Harpes had murdered the night before. Knowing that dead men tell no tales and lest Harpe should tell too much he ran up drew a large butcher knife from his belt and cut of his head well knowing he could make no resistance. It was thought at that day that the Stegalls were not much better than men Should be. We afterwards heard that the other Harpe was taken and in the gaurd house at the Garrison at old Fort Masac Stegall and two others went down to see. They stoppd at my fathers as they went down. This was the only time I ever saw Stegall and I formed a very bad oponion of him then thinking him a bragadocia with but little courage and less merit.

General Clark made his Jouney through this country before my day here. I have seen some of his soldiers but cannot now give any particular account of him other than that published.

[p. 111⁵]

Neither can I give any further account than those published of the life of Col Daniel Boone. In 1813 I was some weeks on a March where a son of his Major Nathan Boone stood high both as an officer and as a man.

Col. John Edgar lived at Kaskaskia when I came here to this country in 1805 and died there many years afterwards. Govr. Reynolds knew him better than I had an oppertunity of knowing him.

I believe now I have gone through all the particular questions you asked. You will also see that I am not a classic Scholar nor even a Scholar of any kind from the disconnected manner in which I have written this communication. Therefore you Excuese the want of proper application of the English grammer there being none taught in the Cane brake where I grew up. Could I see, I might be able to narrate incidents that you might make some thing out of in relation to the setling the country about the Ohio River where I lived, about the setling of this country and something about the commencement of the late war in 1812.

My wife came here some two years before I did. We married here within three of this place in 1809 and lived here abouts ever since. My first wife still living. If you can make any thing out of this communication and can think of any thing else that would be of use to you write and I will try again and try to be more prompt in aswering.

Yours respectfully
J. Lusk

Letter from George C. Lusk

Edwardsville Ill.
October 27 1869

Mr Lyman C. Draper
Madison, Wis.
    Sir. Your favor of 1st inst. addressed to my father, John T Lusk, was received by me in due time. My father died Dec. 22, 1857. He has no brother or sister living, but there are living, the descendants of four of his sisters. I think he had but one brother, and he died young. My grandfather's name was James Lusk. I believe this is all the information I can give, in relation to the subjects referred to in your letter.

    We have a relative, residing about 12 miles from this place, named Henry H. Good, Who came from the same country as our parents. He is an Old time man, and much like my father was, in tracing men, and the deeds of men, who were in any way noted in his earlier days. I have delayed writing to you, hoping this Relative would be in town, intending to talk with him, and make such inquiries

as you have presented. I shall make it a point, to converse with him the first time he is here, and if such conversation elicits any information worthy of note, will communicate it to you in another letter.

        I am very respectfully
        George C. Lusk

Sketch of the Life of Gen. Samuel Whiteside
By Judge Joseph Gillespie,
of Edwardsville, Ill.

THE REPUBLICAN
O. S. Reed, Editor
Edwardsville, Oct. 24, 1877. (Illinois.)

Sketch of the Life of Gen. Samuel Whiteside by J. G.

The first that we hear of the name of Whiteside, is in Ireland. It is a family of note there, to this day. A Chief Justice of Ireland, recently deceased, of that name, was a very talented and distinguished man. The branch to which Gen. Samuel Whiteside belonged emmigrated to North Carolina, and from thence removed to Kentucky in the year 1790. Two brothers, William and John, came to Illinois, reaching Hull's Landing on the 1st day of January, 1793. Reynolds in his history of Illinois, on page 151, says: Illinois received in 1793 a colony of the most numerous, daring and enterprising inhabitants that had heretofore settled in it. The Whitesides and their extensive connections, the Griffins, the Enochs, the Chances, the Musicks and the Goings, and others, were born and raised on the frontiers of North Carolina, and emigrated to Kentucky and were used to Indian fighting and the hardships incident to frontier life. The patriarch and leader, William Whiteside, had been a brave soldier in the Revolutionary war, and was in the celebrated battle of King's mountain. His brother John likewise nobly performed his duty in the same service. Reynolds sums up the leading traits in the character of the Whiteside family by attributing to them the possession, in an eminent degree, of the qualities of courage, and patriotism, and says they inherited much of the Irish character. They were warm hearted and impulsive. Their friends were always right and their foes always wrong in their estimation. If a Whiteside took you by the hand, you had his heart. He would shed his blood freely for his country or his friend. The brothers, William and John, soon took the lead in Indian fighting. William erected a fort called Whiteside's Station, and John settled and died at Bellefountaine. And as the Indians began to commit depredations, the Whitesides stood ready to pursue and punish them. The above named locations were both in Monroe county, and near to where Waterloo now stands, and on or near the line of travel between Kaskaskia and Cahokia, and contiguous to the first American settlement in the county, to-wit: "New Design."

It was not long before the Whitesides had business on their hands. In 1793 the Kickapoos, under their celebrated chieftain, Pecon, stole a number of horses in the American bottom near the residence of a Mr. Miles. Only eight of the citizens could be got together to pursue the marauders. The Whitesides and Col. Samuel Judy were of course among the number. William Whitesides led the company. The Indians numbered about forty-five. They were energetically followed night and day, and overtaken on Shoal creek and completely surprised and their Chief taken prisoner and he gave his gun to the captain. The rest of the band fled. When old "Pecon" discovered that he had been captured and defeated by only eight whites, he called upon his followers to return and attempted to wrest his gun from the captain, who was a powerful man and retained it. In the melee Pecon escaped, and the whites discovering the predicament they were in, after gathering up the stolen horses, made all haste back to the settlements. And well it was for them, for Pecon rallied some seventy warriors and pursued with such hot haste that he and his followers were at the heels of the whites when they reached the settlements. They would have been exterminated if overtaken.

In 1794 the Indians in a most barbarous manner shot one Thomas Whiteside, and butchered and tomahawked a young son of the captain while at play near the station. This of course increased the bitterness and hostility of the whites and especially the captain, towards the Indians. In 1795 the captain was informed that a camp of Indians had established themselves on the bluff a little south of where the McAdamized road between St. Louis and Belleville runs, and that they contemplated killing him and stealing horses. The old hero's blood was raised and he assembled his trusty followers to the number of fourteen, amongst whom were the Captain and his two sons, William B. and Uel, Samuel Whiteside, William L. Whiteside, Johnson J. Whiteside, Samuel Judy and Isaac Enochs. Just before daylight the camp was surrounded and all the Indians killed but one, who made his escape. He was afterwards put to death by his tribe for running away. In this affair the Captain and his son, Uel, were wounded. The Captain was supposed to be mortally hurt, and fell to the ground, exhorting his men to fight bravely.

His son, Uel, was shot in the arm. On examining the Captain, Uel discovered that the ball which, it was supposed, had gone into his body, had struck a rib and glanced off towards the spine, and he exclaimed: "Father, you are not dead yet," and cut the bullet out with his

[p. 114]

butcher knife. Upon which the old gentleman jumped to his feet and exclaimed: "Boys I can still fight the Indians." The shot which the old gentleman received stunned as badly as if it had been a deadly one. As they returned to the station, they halted at Cahokia to dress the wounds of the Captain and his son, Uel. They stopped at the house of an American widow lady named Raines, who had two beautiful daughters to whom the young Whitesides made love, which ended in the two brothers marrying two sisters. Thus far we have been considering the two families of William and John together, and the closest intimacy always subsisted between them. The sons of William, so far as I have been able to learn, were William B., Uel, and John D. The two former lived and died in Madison county, Ills., and the latter in Monroe. William B., or Bolin, as he was generally called, was Sheriff of Madison county, and John D. was Treasurer and Fund Commissioner of Illinois. They were both men of excellent natural talents, but defective in scholarship, as must needs be, considering the period in which they grew up in Illinois. The children of John Whiteside were Samuel, the subject of this sketch, William L., Joel and Thomas (sons) and Sarah and Margaret, (daughters) one of whom married Samuel Judy and the other, Johnson J. Whiteside. Samuel Whiteside, true to the traditions of his family, engaged ardently in the war of 1812, at which time he lived in Madison county, having with his brother Joel, removed from Monroe in 1805, according to statement given to me by his son, although Reynolds, in his history of Illinois, fixes the time in 1803. At all events, they located near the Cantine creek in the vicinity of Collinsville. Samuel's hatred of the Indians was stimulated by an adventure he had in his boyhood. He was with his brother and cousin playing when they were killed, as heretofore stated. He was very fleet of foot, and as the Indians fell upon the others, he started for the house, in the way to which was a brush pile, which he leaped over and the savages had to go around, by which means he got time enough to just escape their tomahawks. This, of course, was not calculated to increase his love for the Indians. The very sight of one aroused his anger to the highest pitch. He engaged ardently in the Ranging service in the war of 1812. Four companies were allotted by the United States to the defense of Illinois. One was raised and commanded by Captain William B. Whiteside, another by James B. Moore, another by Jacob Short and another by Samuel Whiteside. (See Reynolds' Life and Times 133.) In 1812, Hill's ferry on Shoal creek in the present county of Bond, was attacked by the Indians who wounded a man in one of the block houses. Samuel Whiteside's company was the first on the ground, (see life and times 140) and pursued them, but the start the Indians had was too great and they could not be overtaken. In 1814 the Indians murdered Mrs. Reagan and six children in the forks of Wood River. She was returning home in the evening from a visit to her brother, Capt.

Able Moore, and on the way she and her children were butchered. Her husband was at the time doing duty as a Ranger at Fort Russell, and knew nothing of his dreadful bereavement until informed of it by a party of rangers next morning, (see Madison county Gazetteer, page 53.) An immediate pursuit was made by Capt. Samuel Whiteside and the Indians overtaken near the Sangamon river and one of them killed in a tree top by James Pruitt. The rest made their escape by means of the almost impenetrable thickets along the river bottom, but it was afterwards learned most of them died from exhaustion resulting from their flight. After the expedition of Gov. Clark which left St. Louis the 1st of May, 1814, had been repulsed at Rock Island, another was fitted out to go by water under the command of Major Zachery Taylor, (afterwards President of the United States.) On the 12th of August, 1814, the expedition left *Cap au gris*; Capt. Samuel Whiteside, Valle Rector and Hempstead, each commanded a boat. This expedition was likewise unfortunate. The British had planted artilery so as to be able to destroy the whole fleet. When Taylor saw the predicament the force under his command was in, he instantly ordered a retreat. In effecting this movement with the wind blowing on to land, Rector's boat was driven ashore and partly surrounded by Indians, and it was only by dint of the utmost exertions they could be kept off. Capt. Whiteside's boat, being above that of Rector, went to his relief, and after a hand to hand struggle and the exercise of indomitable energy and courage on the part of the men and officers of both boats, they were barely able to get Rector's boat off and save the men. By lashing Whiteside's boat alongside that of Rector's, it could be used to draw the latter one from shore. This movement redounded very greatly to his (Whiteside's) credit for courage and good judgment in emergencies. (See Struve & Davidson's history of Illinois, 281.) Capt. Samuel Whiteside commanded a company in the first and second of Edward's expeditions to Peoria in 1814, in which he conducted himself to the entire satisfaction of the officers who were placed over him and the men under his command. Samuel

[p. 115]
Whiteside resided in 1827 temporarily in the Galena country and upon the breaking out of what was called the Winnebago war, organized a company of scouts and scoured the country between the lead mines and the Wisconsin river without meeting with Indians for the reason that they had fled ... which the whites did not know until this scout made it apparent. He commanded the Spy battalion in the campaign

against Black Hawk in 1831, and had the entire command of the forces sent against the Sac and Fox Indians under Black Hawk in 1832.

In both commands he displayed his usual judgment and courage. It was in this last service that he acquired the title and rank of Brigadier general. This is a brief enumeration of his services in a military capacity. He never put any value upon promotion in civil life he seemed indeed to despise it. He could undoubtedly have succeeded to any civil place in his county if he had striven for it. He did however act as one of the commissioners who selected Vandalia for the seat of government of Illinois, and I think aided in the selection of the Canal lands. In matters of religion he sided with the Baptists, and in political affairs he co-operated with the Democrats. He was an honest man, and the only thing that he seemed to be afraid of was being in debt. He believed with all his power that what he believed was right, and it was rather a hard task to convince him that the opposite side might seem to be right. He thought there was but one right side to a question, and that all honest men would be apt to see it in the same light. He was a famous hunter, and followed the chase so long as his strength permitted. He was thoroughly versed in woodcraft, and knew all the haunts and habits of wild animals to perfection. He loved to take long hunts and live in camp for weeks together, and eat nothing but game. His hunting dress in early life was buckskin, and wore moccasins while in the woods. It would have delighted him to attack a Lion, or Tiger, or Grisley bear. I believe he would have gone into the fight with as little dread as if he had a rabbit to contend with, and I have no doubt he would have employed the skill and means in every instance to enable him to come out without any risk or a scratch. The writer knows of his killing three Panthers on one occasion, and he did not seem to think he had performed a feat worthy of mention. He died on the 3d day of January 1866, one and a half miles east of Mount Auburn, in Christian county Ill., at the house of a son-in-law named John A. Henderson, with whom he had been living since 1855. Whiteside county I have no doubt it was named in his honor. According to Pecks Gazeteer published in 1837, the county was formed in 1836, and he was the only Whiteside of any note in those days. John D. had not then attained any distinction.

[Handwritten note:] Hon Jos. Gillespie, of Edwardsville, the writer of the preceding sketch, went to Illinois & settled there in 1819. In sending the Whiteside sketch, he writes Decr. 20, 1879: "I send you a paper containing a sketch of the family & history of Genl. <u>Samuel White-</u><u>side</u>, since writing which I find it is inacurate in one re-spect, & that is: I say that the two sons of old <u>William</u> <u>Whiteside</u>, the uncle of <u>Samuel</u>, married the two daugh-ters of Mrs. <u>Raines</u>: I was led into that error by Gov. Rey-nolds' book. It is strange that he should have made a mistake in that respect, for he was intimate with the <u>Whiteside</u> family, one of his brothers, <u>Robert</u>, having married a daughter of Bolin Whiteside."

INDEXING NOTE

Page numbers used as locators in the index refer to those written on the pages of the original manuscript, which appear in the microfilmed edition of the manuscript of Volume 1Z. These numbers also correspond to the page numbers appearing in brackets in the transcript.

Every occurrence of all personal names appearing in Volume 1Z is indexed, using last, first, and middle names when available. When only a last name is used in the manuscript, the first name is supplied in brackets when it can be determined with reasonable certainty from other sources. Titles such as military rank, academic degree, or political office are used with personal names only if no given name is provided in the manuscript. If neither given name nor title is available, the person is indexed as e.g. Mr. or Mrs. at the surname.

The original spellings of personal and place names are preserved in the transcription. Such spellings frequently vary. In the index, spellings of these names are normalized to the most commonly occurring variants of the full names, with alternate spellings being given in parentheses at the main heading for the name. Other variant spellings of names, if these appear elsewhere in the alphabetically arranged index, are cross-referred to the main heading for the name. (Double posting is used for variant spellings of infrequently occurring names.) Word-by-word sorting has been employed in ordering the index headings.

INDEX

A

B

C

Made in the USA
Middletown, DE
07 June 2023